THE THROWAWAY KIDS

By: Jonathan Masters

For my father, grandfathers, and father-in-law.

Men who had the wisdom to see the world for what it is, discerned how it could be better, and had the courage to make a difference.

For my wife, mother, grandmothers, and mother-in-law.

Women who believed and supported the ideals of their men, championed them in difficult times, and strengthened their resolve.

For my children.

You gave me no other option than to leave you a better world than the one I found.

Thanks and glory be to the Creator God of the universe. In His image, we are fearfully and wonderfully made, and His providence sustains us daily with the breadcrumbs of His Word.

Throwaway Kids (thrō ə-wā′ kĭdz) *n.* The children and adolescents who have been thrown out of class, thrown out of school, thrown out of their home, thrown in jail, only to be thrown back on the streets.

Q1: Is this a true story?

This story is fiction inspired by experience. The names have been changed to protect the guilty, but the emotions and impact remain intact.

Q2: Could the descriptions in the following pages be happening right now?

Most definitely.

Q3: Will things like this continue to happen?

Without a doubt. Broken young men are not being fixed within prison walls. Outside, they have no real opportunities.

Prologue

"I'll kill you, motherfucker!"   *C R A S H ! ! !*

I didn't find out the details until the police had taken both students away in handcuffs. Donald, 18, had thrown a pencil at Kevin, 17, and it poked a hole in Kevin's cheek. Kevin, stunned, didn't react, and the bell rang. A social worker caught Kevin in the hall and took him for their weekly meeting.

Sometime during the meeting, Kevin became very anxious about something he left in Mrs. Schwartz's class. Kevin hurriedly walked down the hall ahead of his social worker and knocked on Mrs. Schwartz's door. By the time Mrs. Schwartz opened the door an inch, it was too late.

Kevin knocked her over pushing the door open. Kevin used a teaching desk to elevate, landing on his target and a teaching assistant. Sitting on Donald's chest, Kevin rained down punches to the face. Normally brash and bravado-tongued, Donald curled into the fetal position to absorb the impact. Mrs. Schwartz and Mrs. Henry, small women in their mid-fifties, pulled Kevin off enough to let Donald escape. Donald ran out into the hall with the girls from the classroom and was taken to the office.

When I showed up, Mrs. Schwartz's door was closed, and the principal, Ms. Manning, stood guard. I gave Ms. Manning a wave to show her I had run down the hall to help and would be returning to my classroom. She held up one finger, indicating I should wait. Ms. Manning cracked the door slowly, and once again, it was too late. A 220-pound raging teenager came barreling into my chest. I bear-hugged him, hanging on for dear life. When I got my feet back under me, I made sure his arm was pinned against his side; I didn't want an elbow to the face. The principal had a similar stance on the other side, as our physical management procedures dictated.

Beginning to catch my breath, my mind frantically recalled references to our physical training when Mrs. Henry, a bystander teaching assistant, said, "you have to take him to the ground." Before I could respond, Ms. Manning was behind Kevin letting his arm free and clinging to his waist in a desperate attempt to pull him to the ground.

Kevin stood like a tree. I clung to him, bracing myself for this bull to buck. Luckily, the focused, crazed stare left Kevin's eyes for a fleeting moment, and he sat down.

It was quite a silly sight. Our principal, dressed in slacks and a frilly blouse, sat on the tile floor with legs wide and arms wrapped around the man-child in her lap. While Kevin contemplated how he was going to proceed, I stayed standing while holding his arm taught at the wrist and motioned to the principal that she should wrap Kevin's other arm before he hit her.

Kevin reengaged the struggle, "I'm gonna kill that motherfucker. I'm gonna KILL HIM!" The staff stared blankly, not sure who or where 'that motherfucker' was.

Once again, someone outside of the restraint advised, "you need to roll him," and the principal began to comply. I tried to pull Kevin's arm to start the roll, and the principal rocked her hips to force Kevin to one side, but Kevin was rooted. After three attempts, Kevin was rolled half way and sprang back quickly. He slipped his arm away from me, and somehow, the principal was sitting on top of a face-up Kevin with his arms clenched across his body. Ideally, he should have been face down.

Ms. Manning and I each grabbed an arm and leaned on Kevin's chest slightly so that he wouldn't strike us and couldn't get up. Manning and I exchanged a grave look that indicated this restraint went terribly wrong while hoping we weren't crushing or suffocating this disturbed young man.

Donald was charged with battery for throwing the pencil. Kevin was charged with aggravated battery because the teaching assistant he landed on was hospitalized. An MRI showed she had a partially torn MCL where Kevin landed on her.

Ms. Manning had several bumps and a strained right shoulder for her efforts, and Mrs. Schwartz reinjured the left knee she had just finished rehabbing over the past six weeks of physical therapy.

At the end of the day, the staff congregated to discuss the incident. Ms. Manning led the discussion with, "gosh that was terrifying. I'm glad Kevin was so focused on Donald, or some of us could have been seriously hurt. Jon, thank you getting down there when you did. I don't think we could have subdued him or calmed him without you. He could have been running wild."

The crisis interventionist chimed in, "Yeah and thank God Franko was in my office. Can you imagine if Franko would have been in the room? He would have gone after Kevin because him and Donald are tight."

Principal: "that would have been horrifying."

Interventionist: "I know."

The conversation prattled on this way for 15 minutes. No alternative action was discussed. No plan was made for a future incident such as this. We never rehashed our physical management system or how our takedown could have been improved. In short, nothing changed. Two students were sent to jail. One staff was sent to the hospital, while two others filed workman's comp claims. And the same thing could happen tomorrow.

Welcome to the Madhouse.

Day 1

The sky is a blue so majestic, if it were the ocean, I would be able to see 30 feet to the bottom teaming with life. White cotton clouds stretch into the sea soft and inviting as a down pillow. How I wish to be lazily swinging in a hammock enjoying the glitter of the sun through the leaves.

The glistening silver of the razor wire atop a 15 foot chain link fence pulls me away from this bliss as I realize with acute fright I am about to walk into prison.

Two inches of reinforced steel door keep me on the freedom side of the facility. A young man in the control room walks to the bullet-proof Plexiglas and speaks through a sliding drawer, "you must be Mr. Masters. Sign in there," he points to a shelf of three-ringed binders, "and I'll buzz you in. Oh, and here's a bag for your lunch. Only clear plastic."

I awkwardly transfer my containers out of my brown grocery bag into the bag provided, sign in holding the now useless, illegal bag gingerly, and pull at the door which makes a clang-thud impeding my entry. Metal-on-metal, I hear the grinding gears of moving pieces. As I pass through to confinement, I see the one-inch wide by three-inch high latch in the door ensuring that those who pass are permitted to do so.

In the next chamber waits a uniformed guard sitting at a folding table talking to an older, robust gentleman with a white beard and a beige hat. "Hi Jon! I'm Mr. Santarini. I'll be your escort for the day." Turning to the guard, Santarini bids him farewell. "Bye, Jack. It was nice catching up."

We progress through another impenetrable door and meet up with the guard who greeted me, still standing two feet higher than us, behind one inch of tempered glass. Santarini places a inch-and-a-half ovular, copper disc on a pull-out drawer. "3-6-7, Mr. James!" James takes the disc and hangs it on one of three turnstiles full of keys. "Thank you!" With Santarini equipped, we head deeper into the labyrinth.

Santarini breaks the silence when we get outside. I'm too busy stealthily looking around every corner for shadows to notice a lull in the conversation. "When you get your chip (this must be the copper disc), you will give it to the guard up front, and they'll give you your keys. Never, ever, ever take your keys home. They have to lock down the facility until they are found, and you'll definitely get written up if that happens."

We stroll down a sidewalk, between two dilapidated buildings "On your left is the powerhouse and on your right is property. Boy's Home is the oldest juvenile facility in the state. It has been around for 110 years." Santarini's demurely turns into a docent. "Up until about 50 years ago, the facility was completely self-sufficient. There were no fences, and the boys farmed acres of land. That's what they ate." He points passed the powerhouse. "That building used to be the slaughterhouse, used to raise cows and chickens. The only supply truck in or out was a propane tanker about every four to five months. The boys worked the land and supplied themselves everything else."

"That's incredible!" I interject encouraged by the cooperative sufficiency of my new surroundings, "Do they still have programming like that?"

"Oh, God no!" Santarini guffaws at such an absurd question. "The clientele has changed. It used to be that parents could drop their kids off for up to three days if they felt like it. The boys were respectful and had discipline. Now, the boys just want to lie in their bunk and sleep 14 hours a day until they get released. It is an ordeal to get them to tidy their rooms and make their beds, and they only live in a six-by-nine. Plus, it is a liability. The tools can be used to hurt others or themselves. The facility won't take the risk." He nods up to the left. "This is the school."

We've walked about a third of a mile. "Do you do this every day?" I ask.

"Have to," Santarini illuminates. "Not allowed to get rides because the vans have to be free for security purposes. You can only get a ride with a doctor's note. Without a note, you can get disciplined, and Mr. Hicks loves a good write up." Santarini gives a devilish smile as we proceed through the doors.

"Jon, can I call you Jon?" We're already fast friends. "This is the education office. Here are mailboxes. You'll get one, eventually. They are not exactly in alphabetical order, but close. Here is the copy room. You know that is Mike's office, and next to it is our secretary, Pamela's office."

We walk toward a door opposite our entrance. Santarini seems to enjoy his role as host, "Right here is our shared computer. If you want to check email or use the internet, this is where you go. You'll need a login which you probably won't get for at least a month. Things happen slow around here."

Having worked in under-resourced schools, even I'm a little dismayed by the "shared computer" statement and push for clarification. "Aren't there computers in our classrooms?"

"Not in all of them, and they are divvied out by tenure. So, I'm afraid you probably won't get one. But don't be jealous. The classroom computers are over 10 years old, have no internet, and no printers."

Santarini's glib explanation pushes me beyond disbelief. "You're saying we all have to share one computer with internet, email, and printer?"

"Yup." Santarini leaves space for this to settle as he exits the office.

"Over here is the teacher's lounge." The staleness of poor circulation combined with a plethora of exotic dishes from years past motivates me to take note of other possible dining locations as we proceed. "We eat lunch here and play cards. Do you know how to play bridge? We have been looking for a fourth. You can join us!" There is no invitation, and thus, no opportunity to decline. Plus, Santarini is old enough to be my grandfather, and I have fond memories of my parents waiting up for my grandparents to arrive from out of state at nine o'clock in the evening and staying up well past midnight playing pinochle. I guess I will see what all the fuss is about.

"This is our refrigerator and that one is for security supervisors. Do not use it because they get very upset." Santarini opens an avocado green door to reveal warped, stained shelves. Despite three containers of baking soda, a putridness hits me, and I can't help but wonder, *is the salad drawer full of water?*

Santarini answers my thought. "Yeah, the freezer leaks and runs down the back. We empty it once a week." I silently vow to eat peanut butter for the rest of my career. I cannot afford to have a side of mold with every meal 'til I retire (or die).

We pass what looks like the first microwave oven to ever come off the assembly line and one next to it that could be even older. They both have a rotary dial and doors that open top to bottom. One is divided in half by a metal shelf. "This is the men's room." Santarini uses his key to open an adjacent door.

"Good. I have to go." It's not an emergency, but I need a moment to process the decrepitude of my latest career choice. I enter to find rust-colored tiles and a privacy divider wall that has oxidized in an arching pattern for three inches away from every screw-joint. The browns continue to run from the floor up the side of the once blue wall give the impression that the tiles are contagious and have eaten a solid foot of the wall. The wall sways from the breeze as I pass.

Of the four urinals, the one furthest right is missing the top valve and piping. It's covered with an iron stopper but is steadily leaking onto a clear trash bag that is funneling the stream into the toilet. It is perplexing that it doesn't overflow. As I finish, I realize due to the discoloration pattern on the trash bag that this has been the order of things for quite some time. It explains the acrid, humid atmosphere. I attempt to wash my hands in freezing water and pump an empty soap dispenser to no avail. I'm adopting the impression that this place is actively and methodically trying to shorten the staff's life expectancy to reduce the pension obligation. It just might work.

Santarini leads me back through the office and up a set of stairs next to the school entrance. "When the youth enter and leave the building, they line up on those two lines by house, Side A and Side B. Then they follow this line up and go around to the classrooms in a clockwise motion. Before we had the lines, it was madness. Mobs of kids would block the halls twenty at a time. The line gives them structure and something to follow. It's not perfect but it's better."

"This will be your room, 208." He peers through the glass, cupping his face with both hands to improve his view of the darkness. "We can't get in until Mike gets back."

13

"Where is everyone?" I have just come to realize that this ghost town is uninhabited, which renews a foreboding sense of dread. I watch too many movies.

"They are all at a conference at State University. Something about brain disorders." This factoid is not relieving my zombie apocalypse nightmare. "I wasn't invited because I'm retiring. We can hang out in my classroom."

"When are you retiring?" I probe longingly. For the amount of education we have, teaching is not a highly paid profession. Many find hope through the dark days by following the light of a promised pension.

"Well, I already retired from the city schools after 40 years there. I used to teach at Otis House. It was a school and residential for kids who were in trouble with the law, the last step before this place. When I first started here, I bumped into a lot of my previous students, and they made sure that no one hassled me here. I got a reputation coming from Otis," Santarini pauses to puff out his chest and punctuate his street cred, "To answer your question, three more months makes eight years here, so I can collect a second pension."

Santarini leans back in his chair and rests his hands on his paunch. "Right now it's," he squints at the wall clock, "8:25. Lunch is at 12:00. I've given you the tour. Is there anything you want to know? Any questions?"

"Mr. Santarini, to be frank, I taught my last day at my previous school yesterday. For the last five years, my classrooms have been lovingly called Master's Madhouse for the rough clientele I accept and attempt to improve. The only reason I even started today is because my original start date was mid-semester, and my previous school threatened to suspend my teaching license if I didn't finish out the year. This was the farthest back I could push it to appease both parties. It has been an emotionally charged couple of months, and I'm thankful for a break, however short." My body reflects my mentality as I slide to a lounging position and put my crossed feet on a student chair. "We can go over whatever you like, or I can thumb through textbooks and stay out of your hair."

Santarini shows me the attendance sheets and how he keeps grades. He points out specific students and tells war stories. "This kid, Arlovsky, is the Polish Prince. He is the hardest working

14

student you'd be blessed to get. While Newman, he's a piece of work . . ." I'm perfectly content to glaze over and listen to the hum.

We play bridge at lunch where I meet Ms. Grimley, a rosy cheeked 50-something woman with a contagious smile, and Mr. Sharpe, a wiry old army vet who pictures himself a charmer and a hustler, neither of which seem fitting.

The afternoon brings a battery of show and tell in Santarini's room. It seems that every object fondled has a story behind it, and Mr. Santarini is delighted to regale me with each and every one.

"Oh my, how time flies. It's almost quitting time. We get the first 15 minutes of the day and the last 15 minutes as break time, and we use them to walk to and from the gate. We better get going."

The return walk to the front gate takes a leisurely ten minutes, and Mr. Santarini and I stand in the anti-chamber outside the fortified door waiting for the horn. Santarini busies himself small talking each passer-by, trying to convince me he is a royal. Santarini explains why our exit must be delayed, "We can't leave until four, Jon. Mike has spies everywhere." He shifts his gaze suspectingly. "He'll use any and every reason to put the vice on you."

I use the time to contemplate my recent career move. But just as career remorse begins to set in, the warm sun of freedom washes away any doubts. It is the weekend, and I can use a break.

Day 2

As I leave the comforts of my car, an intense terror over my new situation takes hold of me. I left a moderately dysfunctional alternative program in a reasonably affluent suburban community with the possibility of tenure at the end of the year to spend the rest of my career in prison. I seriously need to reevaluate my decision making process.

I try to blend in with the masses as I work my way through the security clearance of the front gate. Employees don't go through a gate per se, but there is a vehicle port with double gates that elicits that freedom moment in movies of leaving a penitentiary. The newly released can't just walk through the front door. On the big screen, he has to leave through oversized, menacing gates that coldly close behind him provoking a reminiscent thought of the time inside while contrasting the ecstasy of being reunited with the outside world with the uncertainty of the future. There is always a jarring slam signifying that a piece of the free man was left inside leaving him forever changed.

Refocusing from the daydream, I find that I've walked out of the gatehouse without the foggiest idea of how to get to the school. The door clicks locked behind me; no turning back. I see a group walking a path between two ancient structures and decide to tag along. Maybe I will make a friend. If I get desperate, I'll ask for directions. Don't panic. Play it slow. Be cool.

I find recollective breadcrumbs that lead me to the school. Once between the double doors, I realize I don't have the keys needed for entry. No turning back now. I wait in the alcove, prepared for the jolt my presence is bound to deliver to any dazed individual stumbling into work who wouldn't dream of somebody waiting in such a strange, tight spot.

I don't have to wait long. The school secretary lets me in. She is a woman of 140, and I'm afraid to introduce myself or take her hand because any slight touch may reduce this already withered sight to its final rubble. She looks way up from her hunch and scrunches her nose to appropriately place her glasses and assess this seemingly

16

gargantuan man, "Well aren't you a tall drink of water. I'm Pam, the school secretary." Her voice is spotty at best.

I find a seat in the office, waiting for the principal to arrive. The secretary putters about her work worriedly muttering under her breath. When she discovers me again in the midst her fluttering, she obliges, "Mike will be here shortly," and continues her scuttle. Retreating to her desk, I note the barrage of sticky notes that accommodate for loss of memory. The office is sparse with clinically white walls, devoid of any mementos. It is a hazardous in this trade to display family portraits. The tremor elicited by criminal comments about loved ones can be hard to shake.

The heavens open at 8:10 AM, and the front office is deluged with teachers. Dialing the clock back tenish minutes for the walk, they must have arrived at the front gate en masse at eight. It is comforting to see that my new colleagues take their contracted work time seriously. I don't mind showing up a little early, but I pride myself on being the first one in the car when the whistle blows.

Mike Hicks, our leader, enters winded and overwhelmed. He sees me, and a confused look gives way to comprehension. He nods towards his office in a silent form of direction, and I follow him.

"Jon, are we glad you're here," Mike beams from ear-to-ear. This has to be the warmest welcome I've ever received at the start of a new job. "It seems like we've been talking about your arrival for months. Were you here Friday?"

"Yes, Mr. Santarini gave me the tour," I answer respectfully while standing stoically in doorway waiting for an invitation to sit. The new educator / principal dynamic makes me uneasy. Wanting to make a good impression, I overplay my subordination.

"We were at a two-day lecture," Mike offers, "hosted by State University, about the effects of traumatic brain injury on learning and development."

"Do you see a lot of that here?" I feign interest to make an investment in this new relationship.

"No, not really, it was some very interesting stuff. We had grant money that we had to spend, and this conference fit the bill. So . . ." Mike takes a second to let it all wash over him. It's obvious by appearance he is winded easily. Calling him rotund would entail that he is a large man. Standing at just a hair over five feet with chubby stumps for fingers and a perpetual flush, Mike reminds me of an obese oompa loompa. "Jon, I'm going to have you observing some of our teachers today. I want you to spend first period with Mrs. Stecker, our history teacher, and second period with Mr. Sawyer, our language arts teacher."

"Do you know when you want me to start teaching?" A lump rises over the uncertainty that awaits me. The first day in a new classroom feels like dry heaving butterflies. It is where the over inflated self-view, confidence in idyllic principles, and pure sereneness of a new opportunity get run over by the bulldozer of disturbed students trying to push every limit under the sun and smear their hang-ups and baggage all over my once blanc canvass. I know, this being my fourth school, if I can cope with the presented reality, I will be successful.

"We'll start you slow. The quarter ends at the end of the month, and then we have summer break. It would be easiest to slot you in at the new quarter. This morning I would like you to shadow Mr. Sawyer and Mrs. Stecker. That will give you a picture of how a classroom should run."

Four weeks to observe, wander, and ready my classroom! This might not be the worst decision I ever made.

Mike leads me upstairs to the first classroom on the left. I can tell he is relieved to be rid of me. The gears are grinding on the day's checklist, and Mike seems all business. "Mrs. Stecker, this is Mr. Masters. He will be shadowing you first hour and then you can direct him to Mr. Sawyer's classroom for second." Mike puts his head down and leaves in huff without exchanging any pleasantries.

"You can sit over there." Mrs. Stecker made brief eye-contact when the boss was in the room but now seems content staring at the computer screen while blindly pointing to an area behind her.

I find a chair a comfortable distance away from Mrs. Stecker, the kids' desks, and the wall (don't want to get cornered).

Students begin to seep in at 8:35. Were this my first rodeo, I would have a notebook and do some charting to look studious. After three other behavioral schools, I realize this gesture seems out of touch, and it is best to play confidently aloof and mysterious.

Mrs. Stecker greets the boys much the same as she welcomed me. "Grab a book, grab your folder, do your work."

The walking dead mechanically do as they are told and file into desks. This process is repeated two more times as different housing units matriculate. With each new arrival, more life is breathed into the atmosphere. Apparently, the boys have some catching up to do following a four day sabbatical. By the time the last unit is in, there is a frenzy of cautious chatter. It appears each youth is talking, keeping watch of Mrs. Stecker, and pretending to work all at the same time.

About ten minutes into festivities, an average sized, stoic Hispanic young man hauls off and punches the rather chatty, large, round-faced Hispanic in front of him, "Shut the fuck up!"

The big one sneers instigatingly, "You're just pissed cause you're a tard, stuck in eighth grade." He turns to the class. "This dude is 16 and still in eighth grade. How fucking dumb are you?" To his credit, the smaller one doesn't respond. Biggie's provocative face slithers closer, pushing for the desired effect. When none comes, Biggie takes his bulbous fist and slowly, delicately pushes the smaller kid's chin swiftly to one side. This elicits a response. With a potent thud, the smaller lands a retaliatory blow to the chest. "I'll fucking brain you," Biggie launches out of his seat with a book raised in both hands to hover over the little one who is leaning back, relaxed with a chiding chuckle.

Mrs. Stecker finally breaks her trance to observe the fireworks. Waiting. Waiting. "You gonna do it? Didn't think so. Get the hell out," Stecker barks. Biggie exits slumped, ashamed, defeated.

It is only moments before his return. Nothing is said as Biggie returns to his seat. Opening his folder, Biggie pulls his desk next to another student and proceeds to copy the entire assignment unashamed and unaddressed.

The periods last 90 minutes, and with the assignment lasting less than half, the boys busy themselves playing cards that appear from someone's sock and reading magazines they attain by trading their ID to Mrs. Stecker.

The bartering once again brings Mrs. Stecker away from her portal. Aware that she has neglected me for over a half hour, Stecker gruffly initiates a dialogue, "Mike talks like you're the second coming. Why should I be impressed?" Mrs. Stecker is terrifying in that I'm-old-enough-to-be-your-mother and I'll-beat-you-with-a-spoon-if-you-give-me-lip kinda way. She appears to be middle to late 40's and has jet black Grecian/Italian hair. She is heavy but carries it in a way that shows she was once a beauty queen pursued by endless suitors.

"Well, um," I'm not sure how to humbly, yet confidently, field this question, "I came from a couple of alternative environments. I have experience with physical and behavior management, including two years at a mental hospital," I trail off perceiving that juggling flaming torches wouldn't impress this woman at the moment.

"Humph, you might last," she retorts, sizing me up, "What made you come to this shit-hole?"

"I chose to come." This comment intrigues her. "I was offered a contract for next year from my previous school, which would have been my last untenured year, but I could see that the program was beginning to fail. We went from 22 staff down to 17, and I was laid off and called back twice in the process. I was the only male in a 'hands-on' program, and one of only three people under the age of 50. The school was beyond our control. I knew I'd get hurt or be at risk of losing my job at some point. I came here because I've been in three different alternative environments, and funding wreaks havoc on staffing and programming. This is the only place I foresee as being open and somewhat stable for the rest of my career."

Mrs. Stecker just stares, bewildered. She does not know how to catalogue me. I have years, but I'm not jaded. I had an opportunity for security, and I chose chaos. I'm an anomaly to her. She appears slightly distressed by me. Her only response is a sneer and sarcastic, "Well, welcome to prison."

Mr. Sawyer is a refreshing change of pace. He is in his mid-thirties, roughly eight years my senior, and a ball of energy. His blond and red highlighted, mussed hair, trendy button down, and feux-moccasins emulate the free spirit he presents. I hope we become fast friends. He seems unfazed by the bedlam of class change, inaudibly directing students to their supplies and stations, while giving me his full attention. "Hey! Masters, right? You can have my chair." He shuffles some papers on a precariously mountainous desk and paints on a smile to address the kids, "Open your books to 136!"

The desks are arranged in a circle, group discussion style, with a table and chair in the middle. Sawyer keeps the chair tucked and chooses to swivel to engage students whilst perched on the edge of the table. It tips as he animatedly makes a point, but he owns it, reddened, and proceeds with gusto. Sawyer has a passion for the literature he teaches, and I hope to be the special ed. counterpart to bring stories to life in this facility.

My eyes wander jealously along three bookshelves filled with class sets of great novels. I'm driven to teach these works because one, most of these kids have never completed a book and to be a part of that milestone is historic. The sparkle of the eye that accompanies this accomplishment is priceless. And two, these stories are the only things they will remember when they get out of school. To them, math is meaningless, science makes no sense, and history is a horrible bore. The nobility of crafted characters creates a sense in each of us, even if fleeting, that we too can rise to heroics. These kids need to experience that goodness does exist. The sad thing is that due to their circumstances and baggage, it can only be found, for them, in fiction.

Sawyer interactively and vigorously lectures for a little over 40 minutes. All 12 young men sit attentively and participate reluctantly. Some seem genuinely interested and driven. Most of the youth are able carry the conversation, but Sawyer is conscientious to loft a softball to the less attuned. Each, save one, participates in the discussion. The exception sits sideways, hunched over reading material, refusing to make eye contact. Sawyer leaves the students with an assignment to address me.

"You have an impressive library." I choose to open with a compliment. I think it makes me likeable from the start.

"Thanks. I wish I had more of an opportunity to teach some of them." He is slightly winded with reddened cheeks from the instructive performance. He's slender, though not defined, with full cheeks. This leads me to believe that this may be his exercise for the day.

"How often do you teach novels?" I'm curiously hopeful.

"As often as I can," he beams at revealing a source of pride. "The reading level here is low, even in regular ed. And, the facility has been in flux due to remodeling the houses. We are at about half of our normal population. It makes it hard to get traction with longer works."

21

"Have you taught all of these?" I ask of the over twenty different class sets.

"Most of them. Some are full sets I grabbed from a second-hand teacher store. The price was right, free," Casey chortles.

"How long have you been here?" I inquire in an attempt to gauge the period it took to become this established.

"This is my third year here. I bounced around districts on the outside for ten years," Mr. Sawyer shares with air of machismo. He has been around the block and expects his experience to be respected.

I decide to stroke his pride. "What is the best piece of advice you can share for a new person?"

"Be very careful who you trust." He lowers his voice and head to keep the conversation between us, "I won't say any more than that. I think you should come to your own conclusions about people. Just be very aware. The staff are not always as they appear. Everyone here is out for number one, and often, they can be mean and catty to anyone who doesn't see things their way."

"*Jefferson House: dismiss outside.*" The loudspeaker relieves the slightly ominous tension.

As the boys are leaving, I get the chilling feeling that Sawyer is not to be trifled with just as much as Mrs. Stecker. He seems content and kind but carries himself with a bravado that hints he does not like being opposed. "Thanks for letting me visit, and thanks for the tip."

"No problem." Casey leaves me with a smile and warm handshake. "You'll do just fine here. Just be a little guarded upfront. It's for your own good."

After lunch and a rousing game of bridge, I head back to Mike's office. "Where to next boss?"

Mike, still puzzled by my presence, suggests, "Well, I think I'm all caught up on the e-mails I missed last week. No major fires. Let's do DO's and IO's."

For the next two hours, Mike introduces me to a plethora of paper packets. Each Director's Order (DO) and Institutional Order (IO) is peppered with numbers, upper and lowercase letters, and Roman numerals. The purpose is to outline and define each and every procedure inside the walls. The notables include how kitchen cutlery is to be handled (reassuring); what and how to bring in any outside items (need to know before day one); appropriate footwear, no open toes (I guess sandals are faux pah on casual Friday); and staff meal tickets in the dietary (my students can make me lunch!).

Since the sheets are far from narrative, it becomes overwhelming as the heap begins to sway. About halfway through, I realize by the way some titles pique Mike's curiosity that there won't be a test. This is a legal formality, and most of the rules are common sense. They have to be meticulously outlined because of past indiscretions and the juveniles' proclivity for pushing limits. I relax, smile, and nod confidently knowing that most of this has little to nothing to do with teaching in my classroom.

Day 3

I'm able to navigate my way to the school with confidence now. I made sure to peak over my shoulder at key points yesterday as I exited, picking up landmarks and directions—leaving breadcrumbs.

Mike begins the day by assigning me to fill in all the personnel forms for new employment. This feels out of place until it dawns on me that at every previous job I've done this before I started, usually at home, without getting paid. It is a little unnerving that after three days HR doesn't have any pertinent information on me, but as long as that check comes in a month, I can salute the system.

"Hey Jon, it's a nice day. Let's take a walk." After a little over an hour, I'm not quite finished but have started to cramp, so I appreciate the intermission. Mike leads the way out of the office to a gathering hoard. Thirty plus boys idle in the two parallel lines dictated by the front corridor floor tape. There is a restrained tenseness in the crowded hallway. Mike veers wide of the line, but a passing security officer forces me toward the middle of the parted sea.

Victims of traumatic accidents commonly recall time slowing as they helplessly watch impeding disaster approaching. I feel a similar sensation as I am swallowed by a mass of unknown conviction. I find the eyes containing the least contemptuous anger and excuse myself to pass. My body cannot hold in the shiver as I push the weighted door closed behind me.

We exit the school and cross the street to a building that appears to be slanting. My eyes follow the foundation from one side to the other; it seems the entire building is leaning ever so slightly to the right. Upon entry, the smell of rusted radiators, mold-soaked ceiling tiles, and decades of poorly ventilated must greets us. As I peer into the first office with windows painted shut, I appreciate how updated and renovated our dilapidation is in comparison. "These are the counseling offices. They coordinate the parole board, court dates, visits, and phone calls for the youth. To your right are the mental health interns' offices." I glance down an adjacent wing that can only be described as haunted. Examining the doorway connecting

24

the two structures reveals a pronounced crack in the floor, which supports my hypothesis that one or both of these buildings are sinking.

We continue to a door that is set into a ribbed, curved wall. Peering out the window I see we are about to enter a gigantic, half-cylindrical structure. "This is the Q-hut," Mike explains. "Building trades and woodshop hold classes back here." Having roots in the rural Midwest, I know the "Q" is short for Quonset. During World War II, these half tin cans were made as airplane hangars. They were left open on both sides so planes could enter one end and leave the other. Most are only large enough to fit three or four planes. If you're passing through the area, take notice; there are a lot of them blanketing the Northern Plains. When they outlived their use, resourceful locals turned them into churches and VFW's. My ancestors made theirs into a banquet hall where the entire town (regardless of whether they were invited) would feast and then polka after local weddings. The resourceful folks at Boys Home have used the one they inherited as auxiliary classroom space.

Our tour proceeds out one side of the hut to five working-order greenhouses. Though they are the newest buildings for miles, they are sanitizingly barren. "We used to have a farm and growing program, but the grant ran out years ago." Mike's voice doesn't waver over such a disappointment. It's just a bit of history as we proceed through the tour. "We are currently in partnership with Central University. They want to set up a horticulture program and will provide seed and five grad students to help us run it. I should be able to muster up money in the budget for a teacher as well.

"This building is the old auditorium." We exit the greenhouse to confront a stately cathedral ascending much higher than necessary with elaborately crafted weavings as it rises to the crest, a resolute vision into a past when structures were fashioned for beauty as well as purpose, each material picked for its ability to stand for generations. A single aisle divides a 300-seat hall with balconies in the rear. A full, raised stage framed by a draping curtain hypnotically draws the audience's attention with expectation. "The auditorium was a school house 100 years ago," Mike shares. "More recently, it was used for graduations and plays and chapel."

"This building is beautiful. They don't make things this way anymore. What is this place currently used for?" I imagine live theater and eloquent addresses.

"It's not," Mike levels flatly, "The tiles are made of asbestos. It is currently condemned."

"But it's in such pristine shape. Can't it be renovated?" I plead.

Mike repeats a previous tour annotation, "We don't have the grant money right now."

The tour proceeds past "Boys' Lake" which is more like a murky swamp. It's the only area where the horizon is quaint forest instead of barbed wire. It is a hopeful view.

Mike waves at a couple of buildings in the distance, "That's laundry. That's the machine shop and powerhouse. That's the store. That's old registration," I have come to understand 'old' is synonymous with condemned. Most of the structures are beautiful red brick. All they need are updated windows, some touches of paint, and a roof. When I press, Mike explains that the monies weren't allocated, and now, the raccoons can have their pick. These haunts stand as a glaring testament to the short sightedness of state government while new construction commences.

We pass confinement and the infirmary, my familiar road to school, and head to the dietary. Mike shows me to the one food line which proceeds into a dining area of 20 or so four-pack tables (one central pole molded to the floor with four stools branching around). "You can get one meal ticket per shift that you work."

"Is the food any good?" I'm genuinely curious.

"Let's put it this way," Mike raises one eyebrow to impart, "the kids are the ones making the food 90% of the time."

Our tour moseys from the dietary to a living unit tour. "Each 'house' has two sides; A and B." We walk down one. "The kids are paired up in each living space." A security officer opens a vacant room to reveal an all red plastic set of bunk beds, a round plastic stool and plastic desk with 2 plastic shelves above it, a stainless steel sink the size of a drinking fountain and a stainless steel toilet with no lid. All fixtures are bolted to the floor or wall with a healthy amount of caulk around the edges to expose evidence of any tampering. The setup reminds me of a child's playhouse or Tupperware.

26

Mike has greatly exceeded his exercise quota for the day and with a flushed windedness, rapidly concludes our tour. "Any questions? Good. Time for lunch."

Day 6

Over the past couple days, I have had the opportunity to visit almost every classroom. This is my reconnaissance:

Upon entering the upper sanctum, Mrs. Stecker's rotund, menacingly, big-fat-Greek-Italian classroom is first to greet me. Proceeding clockwise, Ms. Vasquez is next. She has the scent of a woman whose front room has a Virgin Mary shrine eclipsing one wall. Maria Vasquez is the only teacher I have encountered who legitimately does not tolerate swearing, and it sticks. Students who slip quickly glance to see if she heard, immediately apologize, and self-correct. She is stern and serious but kind hearted.

Ms. Brown is in 203. Forty-five, wiry, tall, and black, she gives me the assistant principal vibe. This is her second career, and she's confident she's going places. She has an authority with Mike. Twice this week, Ms. Brown busted into Mike's office and unloaded story after story of student insolence and security incompetence. Mike seems to entertain these sessions with subtle empathy and agreement, never daring to talk back.

Mr. Sawyer is inspired in 204. Then comes the bend. Ms. Spear is sandwiched between the would-be sisters Ms. Peters and Ms. McDonough. Ms. Spear is a short, squat woman who has a hairy mole that hides the rest of her grim mug. When she is not muttering obscenities about the youth, she is counting down the days (17) before she retires.

Ms. Peters and Ms. McDonough were tragically separated at birth. They are both in their late thirties to early forties and are holding gracefully to their beauty. You can tell by their dispositions, in the recent past they hooked and mounted men as trophies. They are both loud and strong. Both are married with kids. Peters has a ten-year-old boy and a seven-year old girl. McDonough has two girls, seven and nine. Peters has a light heart that she expresses through innuendos, both subtle and vividly jarring, perfected by her training as a health teacher.

My classroom, 208, is next followed by another turn. The tutoring center inhabits a myriad of elderly volunteers who educate

28

youth one-on-one. The appeal is really the collections of thriller and street-fiction novels that tutors can lend to their students.

Ms. Wells is a kindly soul who used her tenure to procure the "processing" office. She began her career at Boys town as a high school teacher with only an elementary degree. When standards forced the hiring policy to change, she shifted to avoid scrutiny. She fancies herself a mother/mentor to children who receive a "time-out-ticket" (TOT).

Julie Vargas is the soft-spoken writing teacher. She hides a timid beauty behind spectacles. The boys defensively respond to her as overprotective brothers, and she seems completely oblivious to it all.

Ms. White and Ms. Green are the second pair of pees whose rooms cover the last corner (212 & 213). They are constantly in a flux of frustration and frazzlement, consecutively. Ms. White has a permanent crease in her brow and gnarled hands from writing a library of disciplinary referrals. Sources contend she has not taught in years due to non-stop write-ups. Ms. Green is a cross between a surprised deer and possum, dropped into the class unexpectedly, too terrified to move or call for help. When she gets whelmed, Ms. Green has shaky hands and a twitch in her right eye.

Mr. Tuck and Santarini round out our tour. They are retired from city schools and continue to teach to stave off boredom and death.

I didn't get the pleasure to observe these last four classrooms and feel blessed for it.

Day 7

The week starts with the faint hope of being assigned a classroom and subject matter so I can begin the hunt for curriculum. I appreciate getting to know my colleagues, but after six years of teaching, observing other teachers is like watching golf on a Saturday afternoon, a snooze fest.

Mike greets me with the dismal burden of a veteran on leave. "Walk with me, Jon." Mike puts his bag in his office, and we head upstairs. "I want you to fill in for Mr. Tuck teaching math. He will be at Janesville, the girls' facility, for another three weeks to straighten out IEP paperwork, and I need our special ed. boys to get some math credit." Mike opens a classroom door. "Here are Tuck's folders for each class. Here is a copy of the class lists by period. I'll give you the morning to get yourself acclimated, and then, you teach this afternoon." Mike exits in a whirlwind not bothering to verify that I heard a word.

Inhaling a deep, calming breath, I survey the classroom. Numbers, fractions, and decimals posters with various formulas are scattered about the walls with no apparent pattern. There are several posters of "Famous Black People throughout History." Each poster has a different theme: civil rights, arts and music, movies and theatre, science and technology, and sports.

My eyes rest on the stack of folders Mike has left in my hands. Each and every folder is riddled with graffiti, mostly gang tagging. If I am going to have any hope of maintaining order, I have to give these kids new folders for new beginnings.

Making my way back to the office, I find an adjoining closet filled with supplies. I grab pencils, notepads, and folders. As I retreat back to my assignment, Mike startles me. "What's all that for?"

"Mr. Tuck's folders are pretty beat up and tagged. I figured I would give the kids a fresh start."

Mike clasps his hands and leans forward as if to instill a lesson on a child, "Well, we need to conserve resources. We don't get to order a lot, and we need to conserve what we have."

I attempt to assert myself, "I understand that, and I will keep it in mind. I just think it sends the wrong message that gang graffiti is okay. If I give them new folders, I can enforce the expectations."

"I fully understand and support what you are saying," Mike blows me off. "You will only be in that class for two weeks. Try to make the folders work, and we'll get you new folders when you open your class."

It is probably in my best interest to concede. "Alright," I say misgivingly. I can tell this is going to be a sticking point. I've made my case. Best to keep the boss happy.

I head back to peruse the resources at my disposal. Tuck has two bookshelves full of seven different types of textbooks and over ten different workbooks. I pick through some of the folders in search for clues as to how this absent teacher ran his class. It seems that each student is at a different point in an indeterminable book. I could ask the fine young gents where they believe they were when Mr. Tuck was reassigned six weeks ago and hope for a thoughtful response. Discretion tells me this could lead to confusion, and it is probably best not to throw chum in the water on the first day.

As I sit cross-legged on the floor casually assessing some workbooks, the hustle and bustle of entry can be heard in the halls. Intermittent, "Quiet! On the line! Hold the noise! Stop at the corner!" is discernable over the din of clipped conversation.

I settle on a workbook that covers whole-number basic facts. I figure I can sustain doing a refresher for a couple of weeks. It won't be too challenging, and the repetitive nature builds confidence and promotes focus, which will help me build rapport and avoid problems. The selling point is the pretest at the beginning of the book, which will easily and appropriately level the kids quickly.

I take one workbook to the copy room and make 20 copies of the pretest. It should be easy enough to hand out and explain, and as each kid hits a wall, I can make-up an assignment out of the workbook to alleviate their struggles. Fool proof.

As I saunter away from the copier confident I have a solid plan, I see Mike head for the restroom. Now's my chance. I run back into the supply room to find my previous pile of provisions waiting. I hold them close to my chest with my back to the bathroom as I exit the office and scurry up the stairs.

"Teachers, the youth are in the building." The loudspeaker's crackle prepares the second floor to receive their students. Perched in my classroom doorway, I gaze to the left to observe kids briefly appear from the staircase before they disappear down the hallway, following the tape lines to the first corner. There is relative quiet, and the young men look disciplined with their hands behind their backs. I'm one of the last classes the boys will come to, so I listen to the jostle to anticipate the final turn.

"You're not fuckin Tuck?!" I am greeted by my first student.

"Mr. Masters," I extend my hand. He shakes it. "Nice to meet you . . ?"

"Davion Pierce," he straightens his posture and pushes his chest to enforce the importance of such a name.

"Mr. Pierce, have a seat," I instruct, "and we'll get started when the other students arrive."

Four more young men filter into my room, none as pronounced as Davion. "Mr. Tuck has been gone for a while, so I won't make you figure out where he left off. Instead, we are going to work on 'Skillz Drillz,'" I've transcribed my catchphrase on the board to give more gusto to the filler lessons. "This is a pre-test to let me see what you know, so we can skip it, and what you don't, so we can work on it."

An inquiry comes from a young man with tattooed tears on one cheek, "Where are the calculators?"

"I don't teach with calculators," I explain, "because they don't stretch your mind."

"Well I'm not doing this shit." The young man symbolically pushes himself backwards in the desk affixed to his chair and proceeds to cross his arm to nonverbally emphasize the seriousness of his statement.

"Suit yourself," I try not to be confrontational. Puffing out my chest against a kid always turns me into the loser. It's better to sidestep, "But, then you won't earn any credit."

"I don't give a SHIT!" The overemphasis of the last word indicates he's daring me to come at him again.

We have hit a fork the first five minutes of day one. If I send this kid out, I give the impression that I can't handle my class. In previous schools, I've experienced that 'tis better for everyone if students stay in their seats in their class. Whilst in the classroom, students create less hassles, less complaining, and fewer questions/attentions from the powers that be. I continue cautiously, intent on not erupting a student minutes into my first class. "I get that this transition may be frustrating for you, and school might not be your thing. I will make you a deal: if you sit there without bothering anyone, I won't bother you."

No response. The strong glare Tear Drops was using to assert his dominance has shifted downwards in an attempt to hide the shame of unneeded over-aggression.

"If you feel like doing work, I'm just going to leave this worksheet here," I place it on his desk and quickly move away before any objection can be levied.

Five minutes pass nervously. I keep close tabs on the objector's hostility without him catching me leering. Abruptly, "I need a fucking pencil!" breaks the tension. Weepy wants to be educated after all.

I am working with another student and do not want to rekindle a spat over semantics. "They're on my desk. Help yourself." Precariously, the boy saunters to the desk, analyzes and sizes several options, finds the worthy tool, and proceeds to his seat to work unassisted for the remainder of the period.

"Great work, gentlemen!" I end the period with a compliment to emphasize the importance of their participation. "Please turn in your materials (I've been gifted a wood block with twenty holes to ensure all weapons, I mean, pencils are accounted for). You have a little over five minutes for a break before the bell."

As Teary turns in his assignment, I try to bridge the gap, "I appreciate you finding the motivation to work. I know sudden changes are tough, and you made a good choice."

He grunts, glares, and returns to his seat.

The boys are propelled by the bell. I hurriedly wish them well as they make a speedy retreat, "Have a great day! Quiet on the way to the next class!" Thus concludes my first period teaching in prison.

Day 8

The symphony of unnerving threats and slurs from the hallway is starting to grind on me.

"I heard you got duked up the other day, Earley?" A squat, ghostly youth with a fresh shiner doesn't seem amused and does not respond to the quip.

Continuing, "You off your meds today or something? Lighten the fuck up."

Not getting the desired response, the agitator picks a new target. "You faggot-ass motherfucker. Where the fuck do you think you're going? Don't be stupid, or I'll beat your ass."

I've been teaching this population for years, so my eyes are fully open to the tendencies and capacities of maladjusted youth. The coarseness lies in the fact that the security staff standing 30 feet from my door feels comfortable addressing kids so flagrantly. He can be heard down two hallways and probably at the bottom of the stairs next to where he stands. A counselor leans on a wall opposite the guard with a smirk that lets me know this is the status quo.

Don't get me wrong; I've let loose on my students from time to time, and deservedly so. A curse word could have floated out here or there. For the most part, they've been purposeful and often theatrical explosions with the point of jarring a knucklehead who wouldn't respond to other attempted interventions. Such instances are often very effective and create rapport with youth who can't connect with professionals they feel are stiff-necked and out of touch. If ever one of the interactions would cross a principal's desk, it could be brushed aside.

It's a hard pill to see these kids being bullied by a grown man knowing full well this model reinforces the king of the mountain mentality of the streets. I'm used to having to combat the home and gang life that have conditioned these young men, but this will be a first combatting my coworkers and the youths' professional caretakers.

Two imps brusquely slide their way through the doorway I'm occupying and begin a game of cat and mouse weaving throughout the room. I split the pair with my body and escort the aggressor out.

"Pussy," the mouse yells over my shoulder, and the cat attempts another chase.

I slide square and firmly press the young man's arms to his body. Bending a little to insure eye contact, I advise, "it's time to go to class," with a firmness that lets the youth know there will not be a fight in this room today.

Tomcat shrugs my hands off and glowers with the fierceness of a toddler. I'm twice the size of this kitten, so I let the right side of my mouth slide into a smirk as I let him know who the lion in this jungle is. He blinks first and parts, "I'll catch you on the bricks, little homey," with a devilish grin to his prey.

I turn back to Jerry the mouse with, "I think he likes you," to lighten the mood.

"He ain't shit," Jerry squeaks. "Bitch is always tryin to lift my merch. That's why I keep it on me." He pulls a packet of fruity candies from his crotch and moves to open them.

"Woe, woe, boss!" I explain the expectation. "If I see it, you lose it."

"You can't take shit from me," he challenges as he opens the bag and pops three pieces in his mouth defiantly.

Coolly, I continue, "I won't have to. I'm sure I can find a guard who likes you just as much as your friend and would be willing to search you for any 'merch' you might have on you."

His eyes betray any confidence. Fleetingly, he pleads for mercy. "But, it's already open."

"Not my problem." Seizing the power, "You know you're not supposed to have it at school. You can give it to me or throw it away."

"Why the fuck do you want it?" Aggressive profanity can be quite humorous when it comes from a defiant Napolean.

"Leverage," I level.

Confused, he cocks his head to one side.

"I'll keep it in my desk," I offer. "If you can show me what a proper young gentleman you are for the rest of the period and complete all your work, I may be kind-hearted enough to return your 'merch.'" I can't help but smirk at the simplification of "merchandise."

I open the drawer to reinforce my ploy and to avoid handling something that just came out of his pants, and Jerry reluctantly drops his stash. Closing the drawer, I slightly convulse at the thought that Tomcat wouldn't have batted an eye at eating these trouser treats.

Day 10

I am blessed to live in a beautiful, unincorporated part of a small, suburban town. This affords me the privilege of being on a power grid of just 11 homes, and every time God sneezes, the power is knocked out for three days.

My alarm clock is set to a hazy Christian station to wake me gently. It has a nine-volt backup, but I've never gotten around to installing the battery. Said clock has two alarms and a touchy way of setting them (and the time) that only worsens in the dark.

My wife, Annie, wakes up ninety minutes before me. Our first marital dispute was over her needing to reset the alarm **FIVE TIMES** before she meandered out of bed. We compromised on two resets, and Annie pushes it by muting the second and returning to sleep leaving me to worry if she will rise on her own. Annie leaves the house precious minutes before my alarm rings.

Today, as I role over to get an armful of our two small dogs, an extra sense of peace and rest envelopes me. I try not to look at the clock for fear I will be inside the 15 minute window of my alarm. Having this knowledge, I can never fall back to sleep and drudge out of bed in frustration for trying.

My restfulness is my first clue that something is amiss. Annie and I have stayed up late consecutive nights to enjoy a series we fancy. My eyes drift to the clock that reads **7:23!** I trampoline out of bed and check to confirm that I have 37 minutes to compose myself and drive half an hour to work. I use the facilities and brush my teeth while matting my hair down with the other hand. I let out the dogs so they can do their business whilst I throw on clothes. With one passing look at the hair, I heft the dogs, lob them in their kennel, and I'm out the door. Whew!

It is now 7:32. With some luck (and green lights), I will make it on time.

I rev to a steady five-over-the-limit and the first light is red. Cosmic irony, I know.

Deep breath, calming thoughts, and I soldier on.

My progress is halted by a yellowing red-light and a preceding driver not willing to take a chance.

37

I start to fidget. My knees bob; my fingers tap the wheel; I roll my neck for good measure.

Green salvation! I draft the bumper of the front runner until I can squeeze through on the outside to pass.

I speed to establish qualifying times at certain cross streets to secure my placement at the front gate on time. Breezing through the first check point, I'm only two minutes behind the pace, which calms me. If I can keep it between five and ten over, I have plenty of distance to make up the time.

Smooth sailing to the second check point. With ten minutes to travel six, I begin to wonder why I ever worried. I use the red time to compose myself and re-center. Everything is fine . . .

Once at peace and ready for the home stretch, I notice two more minutes have ticked off the clock. Not to worry; I still have a buffer.

The left arrow gives me hope. My turn next. But as the left turns red and cross traffic begins to run again, I realize, in horror, that an ambulance is approaching perpendicularly a half-mile out.

Knees bob; fingers go from tapping to wringing the wheel with five minutes to go. The tires screech off the line as I jockey for position.

We hit a straightaway, and I'm in the lead.

Right. Straightaway.

I approach a bumper, and it gives me the left lane.

RED!

I can see the gate. My left foot taps, hands wringing the wheel.

GREEN turn on two wheels!

Speeding fifteen over to the finish; 7:59.

Eclipsed by a yellow bus, I try to pass. No room!

Alternating brake lights alert me to the bus's intention to pick up passengers.

I'm halted at a sprinters distance, and there is no hope.

I speed into the parking lot for the same reason an underclassmen runs when he hears the tardy bell. *Will my effort merit mercy?*

With backpack in toe, I briskly but respectfully approach the front door. I hold it for a fellow belated arriver.

When I check the clock, it is 8:01:03. I'm four seconds late. In my panic, I forgot my car clock is about 90 seconds fast. Surely, I arrived within the window given. I cannot be charged for being late because my manners dictated a delay. I rationalize my 8:00 entry and proceed through the portico.

Mike Hicks is lounging in the vestibule as I pass. I smile and nod a polite greeting as I scurry through the search station. There is a smugness about his, "good morning" that is disconcerting.

As I finish my hurried lap through the education office to check my mailbox, I nearly bulldoze Mr. Sawyer who opposes my exit. "Good morning, Mr. Sawyer." I plaster a smile.

"You can call me Casey. And, by the way," I stop my progress to give him my full attention, "Mike wants you to join us for the SBS meeting this morning. It will start in the library at 8:15."

It's 8:12, "Aren't the kids coming?"

"Security delays them 15 minutes. At least, we hope." Casey shows me his fingers crossed and continues into the office.

What is SBS?

"SBS, or Strategic Behavior Systems, was adopted by Boys Home seven years ago. It is primarily run by the education department in an effort to differentiate between youth and adult offenders." Casey has taken the reigns of this round table meeting after informal introductions. I smile and nod at new faces of counselors and therapists, immediately forgetting their names (I really should write them down) and give a brief, singsong introduction that spells out I'm new to the institution but not to the social/emotional population.

"The idea is simple to explain but can be harder to execute." Casey becomes condescending and even dictatorial over the latter. "If we praise the good and try to minimize our attentions to the negative, the kids will change their behavior to obtain more attention from us." Casey's wide-eyed energy veils the contempt of repeating this song and dance.

I try to spare him the full address. "Yeah, my last school used the Father Finnegan method. He said all boys were essentially good and just need encouragement, a verbal hug. Finnegan pushed a three-compliments-to-one-correction model."

"Essentially." Casey continues, "SBS revolves around catching the students in an action we want repeated and reinforcing it. We do that with school store points each period and 'Terrific Tokens.'" He hands me a circular, golden sheet about two inches wide. "When the students do something commendable that we want noticed and repeated, these are used. Kids write down their name and house, and on Fridays, they have a chance to be picked for a treat. Donuts, bagels, candy—mostly anything we can get donated."

"First on the agenda," Casey broadens his focus to include the rest of the group and directs to the itinerary we received upon entry, "I will turn it over to Ms. Wells. She is our 'dean.'" Casey emphasizes the familiar title with air-quotes. "It's unofficial, but she handles our TOTs, time out tickets."

Mrs. Wells merrily takes the baton like a fairy godmother while handing out a spreadsheet that details the "TOT Top 10." Wells offers an explanation to compliment her annotations, "With our quarter ending on Friday, Smith, Jackson, and McAllister have earned five or more TOTs and have received ten days extended sentence. Jackson, a frequent flyer, has gotten two extensions." She pauses, offering eye-contact to any who welcome it, "Encourage these youth to avoid TOTs for ten days straight to earn their time back. The rest have two to four TOTs, so push them to squeak through the next two days, or they could get more time."

Wells wispily offers the lead back to a focused Mr. Sawyer. Ms. Brown uses the transition to slide me an open folder with a tri-sectioned, upside-down trapezoid on it. "The SBS system is modeled on three types of students. Green are the students who are able to function within normal programming: teaching, expectations, and verbal redirection. Eighty percent of our youth fall into this category. The yellow are students who have received one to three TOTs. They need more intense interventions and may need to be removed from class to talk to youth correction officers, Ms. Wells, or Mr. Hicks. We hope this line of intervention works, and they can return to green the next quarter. The red, as Ms. Wells put it, are our frequent flyers. They consist of our five to ten percent who are the most disruptive, aggressive, and defiant. They've exhausted all of the previous options and need a heavier hand like extended time or to be sent to Truman House, our solitary confinement."

Brown's eyes penetratingly never leave mine until she has concluded. She leans back to shift her attention back to Casey, who takes the ball. "Thank you, Lashonda. With the quarter ending, do we have any more kids with 50, 100, or 150 days TOT free?"

Unaware she has been asked a question, Wells offers, "I can check."

"Lashonda, can you follow up and print certificates?" Casey directs the meeting like an executive.

A nod and snarky, "uh huh," accompanies Ms. Browns lopsided smirk.

Mike catches up to me at the conclusion of the meeting. "Jon, I need you to report to A-C-T training tomorrow."

"What's A-C-T?"

He is agitated by the interruption but offers, "Our fiscal year starts the first of next month, and you will need to complete the training before then. Report to the training room at the front gate tomorrow at six A.M." Mike notices my surprise to the time. "Don't worry, you get to leave at two for the weekend. Kinda nice." He thinks he has done me a favor. "You'll have to report Monday and Tuesday as well."

Mike waits for me to acknowledge. "O.K," I offer as he spins on his heel to head to his office. He stops short of the office doors. "Oh, and by the way, you were late this morning."

The feeling of a child sitting between his parents in the principal's office envelops me. The indiscretion has just been exposed, and I squirm under my skin conjuring which response will minimize the consequence. "I thought I made it in the front door at 8:00; just barely."

"Well, you didn't. Next time, write the tardy time on the sign-in sheet and tell me before you report to your classroom. You are allowed two late starts a month, under seven minutes, before further disciplinary action is taken. No big deal this time. Just be honest." With the bluntness of a butter knife, Mike has belittled me and established his authoritative style: nighthawk, always hovering, ever watching, even when no one is aware he's around. I've managed to keep my shorts relatively dry and vow to be here 15 minutes early for the remainder of my career.

Day 11

"Annual Compliance Training," a distinguished, white-hair gentleman explains, "is that magical time of the year when we get to review all the Director's Orders and Institutional Orders to insure we are doing just the best job possible." He peers over his agenda to survey me. "Looks to me like we have fresh meat?" The trainer is in full security uniform with "Mr. Gagnon" stitched to the right side of a golf shirt. Gagnon has the disposition and drawl of a deep-southern gentleman.

"I'm Mr. Masters, the new teacher," I report.

"We're blessed with an educator! Well, I'll have to dust off my professorial chops to give you the full experience." The other three attendees are amused by this. "You see this bullshit three-day seminar is common sense for those who are new to us and stale, never-changing rhetoric for us who have heard it 20 times. And for the privileged few who get to train you fine folks, it makes swallowing a shotgun barrel sound mighty nice."

I'm frozen by the tapestry of articulate introduction woven into disquieting imagery. Not sure how to respond, I decide playing dumb is advantageous.

Gagnon continues with eloquence, addressing only me. "In front of you are some riveting word searches that address topics we'll be covering. You can amuse yourselves while I attempt to find a salvageable cup of piss this place calls coffee. We will reconvene," he glances at his watch, "at, oh, let's say 7:30." His swift exit leaves no room for response.

I immerse myself in the word search to occupy the hour break we're given tostart the day. There is something about it that makes me want to finish first. When I do, I lean back confidently while casually scanning the room. Settling on zoning out for a bit, I perceive no one is up for conversation at this hour. My manager at the coffee shop where I worked in college attuned me to the fact that most people do not have the morning energy or head start on caffeine that I have. He advised me not to sing around the customers until after eight A.M., and I parley that practical advice into not disturbing the peace as my coworkers rise from their doldrums.

After a long solace, the youth correctional officer next to me, Ortega on his shirt, adjusts his hat to uncover his eyes, and I let him start the conversation. "So, why teach in prison? Is it that tough to find a job out there?"

I illustrate my background, and he is surprised as most I've encountered. I have to figure out a way of sharing my reasons that doesn't make me sound nuts. Although, I've noticed there is a marked reduction in hazing if I seem off-center.

"So, you're telling me you could have taught somewhere else, and you chose to come here?" Ortega reaches for clarification.

"Yeah, didn't you choose to come here?" *There is something off about Ortega's face.*

"No way, man. I served my time in the Navy. Eight years. I needed a paying gig without any education. Prison guard for kiddies fit the bill."

His face is asymmetrical. Gagnon's reentry interrupts my gaze, "Don't let him fool you. Ortega is one of the good ones. He just got back from administrative leave."

"What happened?" I inquire as I ponder if Ortega might have had a stroke or some kind of palsy.

"I was working intake with some new twinkie. She hadn't been on the job more than three months, and they pair us in Malcom House. That's where the youth go to be evaluated when they come in. Well, this big motherfucker who just arrived starts hitting on my darling partner. She clams up, and I go to herd him towards his room. When I go open his door, he smashes my head into it, and the rest is a little hazy," Ortega's eyes gloss over at the retelling.

"I was one of the first responders," Gagnon pipes in, "The 'twinkee' panicked and held down the walky transmitter yelling 'HELP!' Security couldn't communicate and was unclear where the threat was located. By the time we got there, blood was everywhere, and Ortega was hard to recognize. Still is." Gagnon smirks and salutes his friend with a coffee cup. "I think the little bastard knew that security would've welcomed any excuse to beat the living shit out of him, so he was sitting a couple doors down with his hands on his head, waiting.

"Javi didn't wake up until we'd been at the hospital over an hour. Fool could've taken a whole year off. But he's back, three short months later. One of the good ones." Gagnon cheers his friend again with a glassy smirk.

Due to the nonchalant narrating of this near-death tale, I realize I have a long way to walk to appreciate the tread on these men's souls.

Day 13

Yesterday entailed a full day of CPR and First-Aid. I think I've repressed any necessary information on how to save a life. Eight hours of monotone, dumbed down, repetitive DVDs is enough to make me think about injuring myself. Gagnon made it entertaining by piping in that this series was out of date; a new one is in print, but the state hasn't gotten around to purchasing it. He closed with a 10 minute wrap up explaining what we're really supposed to do in an emergency.

Gagnon continually peppered the corrections policy that, "no one dies on grounds," into applicable points of the day. He punctuated this with a story about his time in the adult prisons. Gagnon and his partner were doing checks and found a man hung in his cell. By the time they cut him down, the inmate was dead and cold, "completely blue. But, I am not a doctor, so we administered CPR for 15 minutes until paramedics relieved us. They carted him to the local hospital where he was pronounced dead. I cannot emphasize this enough. In state corrections, 'no one dies on grounds.'"

Today leaves me wishing for more CPR as Gagnon distributes, addresses, and then collects over 100 Institutional Orders and Director's Orders. At first I ask questions to clarify the content and spur discussion, but the catatonic response of my peers helps me realize we just need to check the box and move on.

Training reaches its conclusion four hours before our shift is over. Gagnon gives us a 90 minute lunch to break up some of the time.

When we reconvene, Gagnon collects signatures for all our training sheets and presents us with "Certificates of Compliance" to illustrate our accomplishment. "Display them proudly in your work areas," he seethes with sarcasm.

The day is rounded out by rousing discussions of the state's refusal to pay contractual raises. Gagnon explains, "Less than one year after the ink dried on our most recent contract, our gracious governor decided he didn't need to honor the agreement. Next month makes a full year and," Gagnon looks up and uses his pointer to compute on an imaginary chalk board, "the average person is owed between three and five thousand dollars. That doesn't take overtime into account. I can think of a few guys who could be owed close to ten grand."

"How can the governor just break the contract?" I inquire.

"Well, when you sign the checks, you get to decide how the money's doled out," Gagnon snarkily commentates.

"Is there any chance you will see that money?" This issue seems close to the heart (and wallet) of all involved, and I want to contribute an empathetic impression.

"How does that work with your retirement calculations?" Ortega interrupts my line of questioning.

"It's calculated under my current salary, and if and when this gets sorted out, there will be an adjustment with back pay." Gagnon turns to me, unforgotten. "To answer your question, Jon, our union has sued the state and won at the circuit level. The judge has ordered all wages to be put to the correct levels and back pay to be distributed immediately," Gagnon enthusiastically reassures us.

"Well that's good," I offer with confidence. "When will it happen?"

"There lies the rub, Jonny." Gagnon slows his theatrics. "The state's attorney has put a freeze on the judge's order and now has 60 days to file an appeal. If the appeal is granted and heard, it will take another several months to reach a verdict. We will be lucky if we know anything by Christmas."

"How has this impacted the morale here?" I know the answer but hope to pick up insight by gauging their response.

"The generally disgruntled prison employee has used this as an opportunity for social protest, slowing their already mediocre job performance to a snail's pace," Gagnon elucidates.

"And the papers haven't picked up on this?" My dad strongly believes that simple transparency will lead the public to do the right thing.

"That's a hard place too, Jon," Gagnon contorts in an attempt to describe the twisted intricacies of union / state relations. "You see, because we make a fair wage, have a pension, and are paid out of the public coffers, we garnish little to no public sympathy. Should we raise a fuss, the state will paint us as overpaid and unneeded. We will volley back with corruption, oppressive conditions, unrequited spending, and the dismal credit rating of the state. The muck tossing will end with the public even more jaded and generally not giving a shit."

"Well, that concludes your lesson for the day." Gagnon observes his watch, "It is quarter to two, and you are free to go. If anyone hassles you on the way out, tell them I gave you my blessing. I would love to take a write-up with me next month when I retire. Have a great day." With a clown-painted grin, Gagnon gathers his things and makes a grand exit, waving farewell as the shuts the door behind him.

Day 14

"Oh, you're back." Mike greets me with a look of surprise. I'm starting to think he occupies a state of constant bewilderment. I'm not sure if this is from circumstance or diminished mental faculties, and he doesn't leave me time to ponder. "That's right. ACT training switches to a four day schedule next month. I don't know why they wanted you now; you'll have to take it again in a couple months."

"You mean they're going to extend that training? For what?" I can't imagine collecting dust for four days straight.

"They're adding a Strategic Behavior Systems module and a mental health component," he elaborates.

"And they need another day?" I'm baffled by the glaring inefficiency.

"Evidently," We enter his office, and Mike rests his bag on the computer chair, "Listen, I need your grades and hours for report cards. The quarter ended last Friday, and we will be writing them next week during break."

I'm not prepared for this question and don't know how to proceed without sounding incompetent. "How do I submit them?" I inquire, intentionally vague.

"Put the students in alphabetical order by last name, write their ID next to their name, give them a grade, and they get 1.5 hours for the 90 minutes of class they attend each day."

This is the first I've heard of any of this, but on the bright side, it does answer questions I didn't even know I had. "What do the hours add up to?"

"One hundred hours gets them a credit. We divvy it up by quarters of a credit or 25 hours."

I do some mental math. "So, they should be able to get credit faster here?"

"Yep." Mike ushers me to the door with a hand floating behind my back. "Give the list to Mrs. Stecker by the end of the day." The door is closed before the sentence is finished.

48

Since my list of assignments is so short, I hold off until the final bell to give Mrs. Stecker my credits. I want to include today's work to bolster my numbers.

"What's this?" Stecker has the brusqueness of a deep sea fisherman.

"My grades and hours." I think they're self-explanatory. "Mike told me to give them to you?"

"You're fucking kidding! I just finished this shit!" Stecker looks down and away, directing her obscenities at the floor instead of me. "Why would he have you submit two days' worth of work? Why not carry it over? He's such a tard, all the Fucking time!"

I can't help but flush. "Sorry, just following orders."

"Not your fault. Our boss is just a dickhead. You'll figure it out." She fades back to the perch behind her desk, leaving me to excuse myself.

Day 16

It's Friday; it's the end of the quarter; the kiddies have the next two weeks off for "summer break;" my circadian clock hasn't adjusted from the early shifts this week; I don't know how these random past two days of grades should be recorded; Mike still hasn't committed to where or what I will be teaching when classes resume. Pick your excuse. Neither my students nor I are motivated today. To enthuse the lethargic, I post a daily schedule that includes a "get-to-know-you" for the last half hour. Those who fully participate will get to ask me twenty questions.

The plan has about an 80% success rate class by class, which leaves enough participants in each class for some rousing games.

Q1: "Where do you live?"

A1: "The suburbs."

Q2: "Which one?"

A2: "The one outside the city."

I'm intentionally vague regarding personal information. I can muster up bravery in this den of lions with the belief that even if they find their way out of this cage they're unlikely to track down me or my family. That and a previous student from a mental-hospital-connected alternative school promised me all sorts of bodily harm, found my parents in the yellow pages, and gave my mother a ring and a scare looking for me. After a police report and reassignment of this young man to a classroom on the other side of the school (I still can't believe they didn't expel him), I take care to separate my personal and professional lives for the wellbeing of both.

Q3: "I bet you live in Hampton?"

A3: "That's 45 miles from here."

Q4: "Yeah, you live in a rich neighborhood?"

A4: "You got it."

Leave them simmering in an idea that will land them nowhere close to the truth.

Q5: "What kinda ride you got?"

A5: "A Ferrari."

Q6: "Bullshit?!"

A6: "No lie. It's the red 2009 parked outside the gate. Take a look."

An undisputable lie helps propel the conversation elsewhere.

Q7: "No way you whip a Ferrari."

A7: "I got it a couple of years ago when I traded in my yellow Lambo."

Q8: "No fuckin way."

A8: "Yeah way. I come from money, man. I just do this job to give back to the community. You said it yourself, 'I live in a rich neighborhood.'"

The thought that somebody would walk among them for any reason other than the money is perplexing to these young men. I do need the money but consider this a calling, nonetheless. The inquisition continues:

Q9: "You married?"

A9: "Yeah, for a little over four years."

Q10: "What's your girl's name?"

A10: "Lady."

Q11: They don't buy it. "What? You've never heard of a girl named 'lady'?" I defend my fib.

Coming up with unverifiable answers will appease these kids much better than the party line, 'That is inappropriate to share.' I intentionally confuse my answers so when the interrogator(s) discover my ruse, they get frustrated and give up the quest. It's not very professional but incredibly effective.

Q12: "You got a picture of this 'lady'?"

A12: "Yeah."

Q13: "Let us see it."

A13: "Not a chance."

Q14: "Why not?" Q15: "Bet she's a fat bitch?"

A15: "Actually, I'm into more wafey women. You know, kinda skinny and athletic."

Q16: "Would you bang Beyonce?"

A16: "I've never been attracted to her. She's too made up. I like the natural, girl-next-door vibe."

"You're racist." Q17: "You got any kids?"

A17: "My wife and I haven't started trying yet. Depending on how things go here, we'll think about it."

Q18: "Where'd you go to college?"

A18: "I've been to three colleges. I got my associates at Community College, my bachelors in English at Upper State University (Go Sled Dogs!), and my masters in special ed. at Continental College."

Q19: "Does that make you really smart or something?"

A19: "Not necessarily. It just means I spent a lot of money on and a lot of time in school. And now, I work in prison. To most people, I look pretty stupid."

The dance between making an impression to garnish respect and self-deprecating enough to build a rapport is a vigorous samba. I think I nailed it.

Q20: "Who would you rather fuck, Ms. Peters or Ms. McDonough? Ms. McDonough has a smokin body. You know; for an old bitch."

Saved by the *BELL*. "It was nice getting to know you guys. Enjoy your break, and I'll see you when you get back."

Day17

There is something about the regular infusion of fight-or-flight adrenaline that makes the day fly by. Today, I stretch and yawn in the office until half-passed eight waiting for Mike. Without the threat of imminent stampede, the day rolls along lazily.

I still haven't received a set of keys to get in the building, let alone a classroom. Santarini assigned me to 208, but I haven't heard it from the boss and remain dubious. Besides, when I was hired, I was promised a state-of-the-art classroom for online learning with big red physio-balls instead of chairs. Purportedly, they align the spine and increase blood flow to the brain improving productivity. But, considering the only computer hooked to the internet is shared by about fifteen teachers, I doubt that will happen soon.

Vacating the office and ascending the stairs, I decide it is better to be caught doing nothing in a classroom as opposed to out in the open. I meander down the hallway looking for a friendly face. I pop into Mr. Sawyer's room. "Can I hide in here for a while? I'll just read a book if you're busy."

"Yeah, pull up a chair. I'm just wasting time." Sawyer reclines and lazily extends his hands to a relaxed spot behind his head. The look is perfectly natural for him.

Breaking the ice, I query, "So . . . what do we do for the two weeks of 'summer break?'"

"Well," he brings his hands together and leans forward to teach me the intricacies of no-student days, "the first two days are dedicated to report cards. I'm stuck twiddling my thumbs because to accomplish this, Mike needs to hand out homeroom lists. He hasn't. And, we can't access the files until he unlocks the cabinets. The rest of the days you can take off if you have time, or you will be assigned to the various stations of 'SummerFest.' It is our wimpy attempt at giving inner city, incarcerated youth the summer camp experience they never had."

I chuckle at his attempt to narrate a public address advertisement, "What does that involve?"

"Mostly just sports. We throw out a couple of footballs or basketballs at various locations on grounds. The Hispanic kids gripe about the lack of 'futbols.'"

"Sounds magical."

"Oh, believe me, it is," Sawyer continues. "This year we have a much touted softball tournament. Details are a bit murky, but the winner has been promised a pizza party, so the kiddies are foaming with team spirit." He punctuates his point with the swing of a fist pump.

We merrily continue our tit-for-tat, delving into each other's background. I share that broken kids are my passion, and this is my fourth school. I was drawn here for the structure. Casey laughs at this.

Sawyer moved here from out-of-state five years ago. He taught at an inner-city-adjacent school for two years but lost his position due to cutbacks. He took this position three years ago and has made himself a comfy nest.

Casey Sawyer's training is in theater with a minor in literature. He, like all dusty English teachers, believes that stories transcend time, space, and background and can bring revelation to youth who will be forever changed and inspired to make the world beautiful in their quest of lifelong learning. Thus, his extensive library gives the youth ample opportunity along their journey. Casey's bent for the theatrics makes learning quite a production. "After all," he says, "if you teach like your hair's on fire, the kids are likely to pay attention. Might even remember something."

We prattle on like old war buddies reuniting in a tavern until the intercom address, *"Good morning, Boys' Home teachers. We will be having a brief morning meeting in the office at 10:30. Please be prompt."* CLICK.

I look at the classroom clock to determine it is 10:27 and ask my comrade, "is that normal?"

"You'll find we like to fly by the seat of our pants here in the school. It makes things more exciting." With a clear plastic tumbler of coffee in hand, Casey leads the way to the meeting.

"Here are your class lists for report cards." Mike wastes no time with pleasantries as he curtly determines who gets each sheet. I'm left without. "I would appreciate the report cards back sooner rather

54

than later because I leave for vacation Wednesday." I witness several placid demeanors cheer from this news. "Please let me know when you plan to take time off, so I can plug you into the SummerFest schedule. You will be expected to report to your assigned locations at nine sharp and stay until eleven, then back at one, and stay 'til three. Do not let me hear you're leaving early." Mike's glower spans the room.

"The good news is that I just got out of a meeting with Warden Price, and we have a truck of 44 computers inbound for our facility." A cacophony of shuffling sighs and dejected groans interrupts Mike's flow.

Sawyer gets it back on the tracks. "When can we expect to have the classes up and operational?"

"Good question. I'm told we're going to hear bids next week and the following on power and internet hookup. We hopefully should begin the project next month with classes soon to follow." Mike crosses his fingers on both hands in a cheesy display of faith that convinces no one.

"Will we be getting any training before we are just thrown into these classes?" Ms. Brown has a condescending and nasally way of joining the conversation.

"Yes, yes of course," Mike's confidence betrays him. "There is funding for a two-day training with the county board of education. That means training credits." Mike punctuates his enthusiasm with a mock rapid cheerleader close hand clap.

"Yay," Ms. McDonough croaks with an indifferent twirl of the finger.

"If there are no more questions? Good!" Mike does not leave enough time for response as he scuttles back to his office. He pokes his head out for one more imperative, "Please get those report cards back to me, ASAP," and shuts us out.

"What's the deal with the computer classes?" I've latched on to Casey as my only friend and lifeline. If I don't follow him, I fear I will be lost.

"It's a never-ending joy ride," smiling with sinisterly widened eyes and a subtle tick. "The state got funding from City University two years ago to implement an online, virtual, credit recovery program. Staff and youth were pre-interviewed for this experiment by grad students to set up validity. We were supposed to be studied periodically for a year to determine its effectiveness. The program has been implemented in two of the seven facilities in the state for the past several months. When and if we get computers here, I doubt we'll even be studied. The kicker is, if the study funding runs out, I doubt the state will re-up the contract, leaving us with state-of-the-art paperweights and an exercise in futility."

"Not a big fan?" I offer.

"No, not really." Casey becomes snippily angry over the new imperative, "I didn't go to school for six years to babysit a bunch of borderline adults while they learn just enough to punch the right key before they forget it all, to earn a worthless diploma that will do jack for their life prospects," Casey pauses to compose and catch his breath. "Not my idea of fun."

Day 18

Starting the day by continuing my attachment to Casey, I remain long enough to learn the ins and outs of report cards. He shows me a form that appears to have been copied, the original lost, then copied again with this process being repeated enough times for the weather-beaten product to be skewed enough to cut off the top left and bottom right corners. I handwrite two of them, never asking why things weren't computerized, and Casey never offers. Technology (or lack thereof) is a touchy subject. Gracefully taking my exit before I wear out my welcome, I hope to get some face time with Mike.

As I descend the stairs, I plan my attack. Mike appears to reside in a state of flux, constantly flustered. If I give off a leisurely impression, Mike will pile me with busy work. If I ask too much, quid pro quo, he'll ask me for a favor. I cement my approach:

"Morning! Do you have a moment?" Mike waves me in but continues to focus on the mountain on his desk. "I just wanted to see if I could find out what I might be teaching when we return from break."

Mike finds a point to stop and looks up, pen poised to continue. "Mr. Tuck has finished the six weeks we're allowed to assign him to a different facility and will return sometime this week," he explains. "Ms. McDonough will be assigned to Janesville starting next week. I think it is easiest if you just cover her science classes, and when she gets back, we will assign you your own classes."

"Perfect, I'll pick her brain." I rapidly retreat with an expressed plan of action that will keep me in good graces. Putting a cherry on top, "I heard we're having a softball tournament." Mike pauses but remains unresponsive. "I am a certified umpire. I could bring in my clicker and cleats if you want me to officiate the tournament."

Mike raises his gaze to offer me warm eye contact. "I will keep that in mind. We have a volunteer who comes in to do it. He has a good rapport with the kids which helps the game run smoothly. Thanks anyway."

I exit with brownie point in hand, despite not actually doing anything, and pat myself on the back for a pain-free interaction.

"I hope he doesn't think you're gonna be teaching in here. No offense, but I have my stuff just the way I like it, and let's face it; you haven't been tested here yet. So help me God if I come back to a mess!" Mrs. McDonough prays to the ceiling tiles with wrung hands. I don't know if it is my smell or a general contentiousness, but people here get really defensive when I enter their space.

"I would much rather teach in my own space to get the room together," I deflect hoping to salvage my reputation. "I just was wondering if you could point me to any materials as a base for a science class. I'm a big fan of physics." I steer clear of asking to borrow the materials Mrs. McDonough is currently using because 1) her territorial nature has been established and documented and 2) it is very difficult to try to maintain the velocity another teacher has established. Either I go at a pace faster than McDonough and frustrate the kids or slower and bore them. Both cases bring comparison and criticism during which no one wins. *She's a better teacher*; now I feel inadequate. *You're a better teacher*; now McDonough thinks I'm an upstart after stealing her students. The precariousness of the situation is a little exhausting.

"I'm using the books on the radiator. You can help yourself to any of the others on the shelf." She points to a bookshelf overloaded with sets of textbooks and a myriad of work books. "But, I need them back when you're down. Good materials are hard to find, so if you get some, hang on tight." She rolls her eyes to a Sudoku puzzle I've interrupted. It is placed in a file folder that she opens toward the door so as to look productively occupied.

I peruse the collection, gathering a stack of samples. Resolving to make my curriculum selection elsewhere, I don't wish to challenge Mrs. McDonough's dominion any longer.

Day 20

My decision to brown nose has bit me in the ass.

The day starts out benignly with my half mile walk from the gate to the school. As I enter, I think, *I could get used to such a serene walk to start the day.* The grounds are littered with majestic, ancient foliage.

Walking into the office to check my assignment, Ms. Brown greets me. "I talked to Mike. Your keys are at the gate. Go find Mr. Lochte in property to get your chip. Take the chip to the gate, and voila, you have keys."

"Does anyone call him 'Mr. Loch' because of his chosen profession?" My stab at irony is met with an unamused scowl. I have serious doubts as to whether I will ever break through to Ms. Brown. Because of her seniority and administrators credentials, Ms. Brown has assumed the non-existent job of assistant principle. She asserts her position with icy coldness, and Mike plays along because Ms. Brown does the lion's share of his work.

After my second turn on the roundabout, I try my key in room 208, and presto! I have arrived. The stale, dankness of the new-to-me classroom fills me with the warmth of possibilities.

My thoughtfulness is interrupted by, *"Mr. Masters, please report to the school office." CLICK.* Ms. Brown has summoned to let me know that the volunteer softball umpire is MIA, and two houses worth of youth are waiting on the softball field to compete. She seems to take pleasure in denying me a trip to the car for equipment and sunscreen. She off-handedly remarks that the security supervisor's office may have sunscreen while reiterating, "The youth are waiting," with a smug, nasally cadence.

As I hurriedly lather a knock-off brand of sunscreen that just won't rub in, I come to grips with the reality that I'm about to enter a cantankerous arena to boos and jeers and ruin a newish pair of shoes (baseball dirt is immune to soap & water; it will remain for the life of the shoe) to do a job for which I'm neither prepared nor assigned to do, with little chance of appreciation.

I try to remain as inconspicuous as a chameleon, posted up against the backstop. Poor planning has left only eight feet between home plate and the backstop, leaving me with the real possibility of having my teeth knocked out regardless of where I stand, much less if I make a bad call.

The security supervisor who gave me access to sunscreen observes with his thumbs tucked through his belt loops. He admires my foolishness as he critiques my craft. Mr. Vincennes is a shorter, barrel-chested man that reminds me of a black Frankie Avalon with close cropped hair, ruggedly handsome as he ages. Vincennes is a hardball umpire, and between innings, we trade sideshow stories of clowns we've come across in the heat of sporting events.

The spectacle is worth the price of admission. Most likely due to funding, the field is supplied with only one set of equipment. This means that rival houses (and sometimes rival gangs) have to pass off gloves during the transitionary periods of the game; tensions escalate with the passing of each inning. Even more brazen is the metal bat handoff. The materials cannot just be placed on ground for the next possessor. These gentlemen have to bestow their wares with increasing aggressiveness while pausing just short of expulsion from the game. More than one time, a security officer has had to lift a walky-talky to mouth with finger poised as a final threat. Each gesture is met with surrendered hands, flight, and a begrudging, "I'm gone from it."

My salvation arrives in the 4th inning. The much touted volunteer has arrived and will provide me with relief. He has no sense of urgency as he changes his shoes and adjusts his cap. I'm left to finish one more inning, but finality makes the outs fly by.

I resolve to find the farthest station away from the field for afternoon duty as I navigate somewhere to cleanse these shoes in vain.

SummerFest Week 2

The low temperature for this week was 94 degrees. A couple days exceed 100. Needless to say, outdoor activities have been canceled. The blustery union displays the provisions for staff to wear shorts at work. It has to be at least 85 degrees, and the staff need to be engaging youth in outdoor recreation. We are required to bring non-athletic shorts to our assigned area of duty (i.e. the school), change just before the activity, and return to proper attire upon completion. None of this seems to apply to us as we puddle into the school each morning. I don't mind the heat, but as I picture this walk during the winter months, I shudder.

Monday, we are given reprieve as nobody had planned for this weather and the communication network for a last-second change is evidently nonexistent with so many moving pieces. I'm told that security staff assigned to each house will intermittently take their wards to the gym for an hour or two, but teachers are not needed at this time. I am happy to use the time to solidify my textbook choice, plan an introductory day with icebreakers, and start to structure my classes for the coming weeks.

The remainder of the week is filled with alternative SummerFest. The softball tournament has been put on hold with the promise of culmination when the heat breaks (guaranteed the boys will not forget with pizza on the line). Ms. Brown informs the group that we are to report to one of the two gyms for half the day. Younger, more able bodied (me) are to report to the recreation center, and the rest get to stay in the school's weather-warped gym. The youth have tracked 40 years of rain, snow, and salt across a floor that looks to have never been swept. There is not a flat spot to be found as the planking boards look more like the soft waves of an ocean.

Ms. Brown masks a sinister glee as she relays, "Warden Price has banned basketballs from the gyms. The games get too rough because gambling is most likely involved. He wants a structured activity or sport. You can coordinate with security. There are some supplies in the copy room. Good luck!" She can't keep a snide smirk from creeping up one side of her mouth as she orders us to do what most of the grumblers find agonizing.

Browsing the schedule, I've been assigned to the morning shift with the librarian for the remainder of the week. I'm quick to survey the available equipment as I wrack my brain for a creative activity that will inspire the boys to perspire. I spent an entire year as a P.E. teacher for a suburban alternative school. The budget was getting squeezed, and the only way I could keep my job was to teach four sections of gym and two of language arts. The dress-code was a perk, and I survived, but longevity in an undersized, behaviorally-disturbed gym will be left to a better man than I.

I make fast friends with Mr. Frank when he sees me carrying a punctured foam dodgeball and hears I have a plan. I had to use duct tape in a crisscross pattern to give this sorry ball any viability.

Frank and I exchange pleasantries on the sultry walk to the rec center, and I'm interested to find that Ronny Frank is an amateur Thai fighter. Ronny used to be security but got hurt in a restraint and took the librarian job to avoid further interruptions to his training. He accurately fits the profile of a fighter: Asian descent, smaller, and ripped. We share our fondness of mixed martial arts as the conversation leads us into the gym.

The boys are huddled on a couple of four-row risers with security holding up the wall in the corner, oblivious to the youths' interactions. I follow Mr. Frank to make friends. Even though Frank does not don the uniform anymore, he is still very much a part of the security brotherhood.

After ten minutes of introductions and varsity locker-room talk, we get down to the task at hand. It is not in the security job description to spearhead programming, so we'll be taking the lead. I try to wrangle some attention but have no pull due to "who the fuck is this guy" syndrome. Security helps; "All you mother fuckers need to shut it! Mr. Masters has an activity to explain and then you pussies can get back to your circle jerk!" I'm becoming desensitized to the vulgarity of the professionals and begin to empathize a little. With the structure of the institute and the ratio of 30 plus boys to two security, I don't know if I could motivate more effectively without roaring like the king of the jungle.

I quickly explain our one-ball team dodgeball game. It requires a basketball court with players of each team occupying half of the court. Players throw one ball back and forth until everyone is out, but the spice is that once a player is out he roam the opposing team's side and end lines, and if the ball crosses, said player can still engage the opponent, now with no reprisal. Teams start with one player on each of the opposing team's lines, essentially surrounding them at all times.

The first time around we have a dozen test subjects who proceed gingerly, but with my steady coaching, get the hang of it and are soon in a frenzy. It only takes two quick games before more wish to join. Asserting my authority, I kindly tell them they'll have to wait for the finale to join a new game. As a show of respect, I enlist the security guards to divvy the talent.

By the end of our time, the boys are remise to end the revelry. Shockingly, I even get a couple thank you's and have to promise to return before they shuffle to the dietary.

The activity works the same way the next two days, but on Friday, Jefferson cottage cycles back through. At first, they resume where they left off. But, tedium sets in at the hour mark, and the youth need something fresh. Teaching a new one-ball, every-man-for-themselves dodgeball game, I win back the crowd and ease the tense security.

The game begins with me throwing the ball high and far. Whoever reaches it first is allowed three steps before he throws. When knocked out, a person must exit the game and remember who extinguished them. For if (and when) that player goes out, everyone who that player halted may now reenter. The psychology of the game is a great case study. At first, factions arise never thinking they'll eventually need to turn on one another and jail break players they helped lock down. Once the boys get the hang of it, hijinks ensue and each young man reverts to a state of childhood from which life circumstances rushed him through too soon. The game is perfect for blurring gang lines or any other loyalties, and the exhaustion of good hard competition fosters bonding.

We're only able to complete one full game, having to cut the last short due to lunch. Almost every youth thanks me with a smile on his face, and I even get a fist bump from both guards at the exit. Filled with a comfortable affirmation, I think I might make it here.

Day 27

Sleep evaded me last night, and I have a lump in my throat that can't be swallowed as I approach the school. The first day of classes is always nerve wracking whether in a new job or just a new year. Feeling a wisp of nostalgia as I enter, I realize this could be my last first day. Due to the extremity of the youths' circumstances, school is run year-round with only a couple of weeklong breaks sprinkled between quarters and two weeks for Christmas. I vowed to myself (and my wife) that this would be the last stop because I've now taught at four different schools in seven years. Even painful memories can choke a person up at the end of an era.

"Okay guys. So, the crank shaft and the motor are both under warranty." A 'no school today' sign greets me as I check my mailbox. Mike calls for a pow-wow at 8:30. "We can fix the air conditioner, but we need some parts that won't be here for four days. We hope it is fixed by Monday or Tuesday. Today you'll be teaching at the houses. I'll let you decide how you divide up. I want you in the house by nine. Not leaving here by nine; in the house by nine."

I ruminate on my stay of execution pondering whether just ripping off the first day Band-Aid would have just been better. Two teachers leave when Mike finishes speaking. The rest of the room falls to quiet murmurs.

Breaking the silence of a five minute drought, I decide to address the audience, "Well guys, we have ten teachers and three houses: three teams. We can spend some time on each house and switch. Does that make sense?"

"Sure."

"Yeah," both respondents are hesitant.

"Should I draw up a schedule?" I offer trying to make friends through service.

"Yeah."

"Sure."

65

"Okay. Ms. Green, you talk to Ms. White." I appreciate their kinship which I think will win me favor. "Who wants to go with them? Thanks, Ms. Peters. And you guys are going to . . ?"

"Madison!" Ms. Green is quick to pick what she believes is the easiest cottage but overplays her hand a little. "I'll lasso Ms. White and get going."

"Perfect! Madison's covered. Mr. Tuck, can you go with Mr. Santarini and Ms. Vasquez? Where do you want to go?" I'm careful to lump the geriatric crowd together, trying to give myself some time with the cool kids.

Ms. Vasquez responds, "I'm going to Jefferson," definitively leaving out what she thinks of my plan.

"Fine. Sawyer, Stecker, Vargas and I will go to Washington. We'll switch at 10:15 and then after lunch. I'll give each group a schedule."

I draw up the master plan on loose leaf because Ms. Brown occupies the only computer hooked to a printer, and I'm not sure I could gain access anyways. With the paranoid, territorial nature of most staff, I will not be asking for any favors so soon. I purposely leave Ms. Brown to her own devices thinking that she will probably hang back and give Mike an update anyway. Plus, I'm still under the impression that she bites, so I will avoid talking to her until I'm tenured.

As the final copy prints, I'm feeling pretty good about myself. I took initiative, solved a problem, and I think I've shown the teachers that I understand and respect their social circles.

"Mr. Santarini, I made a schedule so we can hit all the kids today." Santa, as he is affectionately (and appropriately) called behind his back, has reappeared. I interrupt his contemptuous small talk with Mike. It's astonishing how two-faced people around here are; even Santa can paint on a fake smile as he chats up the boss. "You are with Mr. Tuck and Ms. Vasquez. Your group will go to Jefferson first, then Washington at 10:15. That way Ms. Vasquez doesn't have to walk far. She can take the van back for lunch, then take a van to Madison for the afternoon session."

I can tell Mike is none-too-fond of Santarini and appreciates the interruption. "Mr. Hicks, do you want a copy so you know where the teachers are?"

66

"Great, thank you," Mike pleasantly accepts my efforts.

Bumping into Ms. Wells as I traverse the stairs, I pause a couple steps up to share the plan. Ms. Wells has no students, per se, being the referral interventionist/coach, but she offers to come with some board games none-the-less. I join her with Tuck, Santa, and Vasquez, which will give each house an even four-pack if Ms. Brown goes with White, Green, and Peters.

Upstairs, I tread lightly into Mrs. Stecker's room. "Steck," I try a familiar tone hoping to ingratiate myself a little, "you, me, Sawyer, and Vargas are on a team. We are going to Washington first."

"What if I don't have any Washington kids?" Her expression warms from contempt to mocking. "Didn't think of that, did ya?" Stecker takes a garish pleasure in watching the air whistle out of my balloon. "I'll be heading to Jefferson to see my kids."

Bruised but not broken, I move to Casey Sawyer's class. A friendly face will help me rebound. "Sawyer, I came up with a rough schedule so we each have a place to be. We can fine tune it for the rest of the week." I downplay my contribution to cushion another potential blow, "This is just a sketch, so we don't all go to the same place."

"Well, I'm going to see my kids for 30 minutes each." Sawyer doesn't even look up as he frustratingly stuffs books into a clear plastic backpack."

That cut deep, disregarded by someone I thought was becoming a friend, someone who appeared to be a beacon of positivity in an all-encompassing wasteland.

Venting some frustration, "So, nobody wants to attempt a plan?"

"Nope. Not how things work around here." Flippantly, Casey blows me off as he continues to take stock of his materials.

"So, it's possible that one cottage will have six teachers and another will have one."

"Yep."

"And no one cares to change that or make a plan?"

"Nope."

"Well isn't this just a cluster fuck!" I get snippy as my composure is lost and the institutionalized side of me shines through. Being around a vile, delinquent population leaves an imprint.

67

Despite attending church every Sunday, anger turns me into a foul-mouthed pubescent.

Casey empathizes, "That's just how things are."

I plead, "They don't have to be, though." He shrugs and leaves his classroom with me in it.

I drag my feet back to the office in a walk of shame. "Mike, it seems that the teachers all are going to do their own thing. So, the plan you have isn't in place."

"Well, you gave it a try," he extends a rare, verbal pat on the back. "So, what's the plan?"

"Well Mr. Sawyer and many others seem content with the chaos and are just going to do their own thing." I can't help but sound childish, pathetic.

"Yeah, that usually happens," Mike offers.

"I'm just frustrated nobody seems to even want to try for something better," I dejectedly share. "Everyone is content with the hole they've dug."

"Welcome to the politics of dealing with a union that would rather assert its stupidity than collaborate toward any common sense." Mike's candid dig makes me doubt my allegiance. "Usually, the teachers try to get a small group of kids, two to three at a time, and teach that way. Use it as an opportunity to get to know your kids. The security will help you locate them." Mike kindly dismisses me with his gaze falling back to his computer screen.

"Thanks." The lesson today has, unfortunately, hardened my shell.

Day 28

The nice thing about felonious youth is they'll reveal their true personality straight away. After just one day, I can list each of my students by cottage and divvy them up by personality (quiet/loud) and skill level (high/low). This, I decide, is the most efficient way to teach small groups in short increments.

My first group goes swimmingly: high intellect, very quiet. We breeze through the four-page packet in 15 minutes. The boys actually ask me to stop reading for them and quietly work. When complete, they rise without prompting and, through eye contact and a head nod with security, stroll down the hall to their assigned rooms and wait patiently for access. I have to reinforce such exceptional participation with some sort of treat tomorrow.

The second group is much of the same. A little mouthier, two youth argued aggressively to the edge of altercation. They finish their assignments quickly and escalate their beef away from my station until security staff, having heard enough inaction, lock them down.

Group three is the low group. My plan is to cover the smarter kids first and ration out the rest of the time allotted with the under-average. Charles is a fitting left-over from group two. He incessantly whined excuses, "I don't want to do this shit. I'm gonna drop outta school when I leave. I don't need this crap," whilst the other group two boys distanced themselves from him with a quick finish.

I use the solitary time between groups to encourage him through gentle motivation, "Charles, if you don't go to school, how will you find a good job? The parole board wants to see you make the right decisions in here so they can be confident you will make the right decisions out there." I know I'm reaching, but I hope my bluff fools him.

Obstinately crossing his arms, "School doesn't matter," he counters.

"Charles if you don't work, you fail and/or get a TOT. If you get enough TOT's you get an extended sentence. And yes, school does matter because the parole board does look at your report card."

Never having written a TOT, much less understanding the credentials of the parole board, I go all-in on my bluff.

"Okay Mr. Masters, I got you." It works! Fake it 'til you make it. Charles mood changes as his new group of less threatening peers assembles.

His upbeat attitude doesn't last long. Charles leaves after five more minutes with a grand total of three out of twenty reading comprehension problems done in 30 minutes.

Moving on to the next young man, I find his confidence unstoppable, "I can do this. I got this. This stuff is too easy." Zion can barely read, but what he lacks in skill, he makes up for with chutzpah. He follows along as I read, and although he offers to read himself, he is unsuccessful. Despite my reading and prompting, he is able to answer only half the questions verbally, immediately asking how to spell them. Despite his extremely low ability, I truly believe that Zion has the work ethic and drive to rise above the circumstances that led to his incarceration. My heart warms as time rolls on. When I have the opportunity to truly help an inspired person, it doesn't feel like work.

Sitting on my other side, a youth with the last name Paris is insatiable. "I can't do this. I can't read. This is too hard." I didn't have the pleasure of meeting him yesterday due to his confinement for fighting. I learned most of what I need to know about him by the droop elicited when I ask the guard if he could take Paris out for school. Note to self: I need to make friends with security to the point where they're comfortable telling me taking a kid out is a bad idea. Right now, their response is that of a glorified butler; 'right away sir,' and I'm unaware of what I'm walking into.

"I'm here to help you, Mr. Paris." As we read, Paris is physically unable to keep his eyes on the paper for more than five-second increments. He looks at me, looks left, looks right, back at the paper, left at the guard station, across at Zion, paper, right, door to the outside, window, me, above me, paper.

His protest continues, "I can't do this shit. I can't read."

"Just follow along. We're right here." Paper, door, suspiciously watching youth passing behind him, guard station, me. He follows my waving hand ball into one finger and point back to his paper. Then, back to Zion.

His head movement is so quick and consistent it makes me nauseous. "I don't know any of this!"

"Well, this answer is in paragraph three." I'm losing patience as I guide him closer. "What did William **Penn** name his colony? It is also a state. William **Penn**."

Paris looks up at me, looks right, "I don't know this shit."

"I don't expect you to. But, I do expect you to search for the answer where I tell you."

"I can't read!" looks left.

"I can't tell if that's true," heating up. "You haven't looked down at the page for more than two seconds at a time. Look where I'm pointing! What was **PENN'S** colony named?! Think states that begin with Penn."

"This one," pointing to 'Pennsylvania' like throwing a dart at a board.

"Yes. See, you can do it," I calmly congratulate. "You just have to be willing to try. Anyone who tries can get an A in my class."

Paris flips the page over to write down the answer. "How do you spell that?"

Returning to school from Washington house, I catch up to Mrs. Wells. "You know a couple of teachers yelled at Red for giving you a hard time with yesterday's plan," she shares.

"Red?" I inquire, unsure of who has gone to bat for me against whom.

"Red, oh I can never remember his name. Casey!" she exclaims the answer.

"Oh, Mr. Sawyer?" I offer, "How did they know he gave me a hard time?"

"Gossip spreads like a virus around here. Just thought you'd like to know that the teaching staff is supporting you." She smiles sweetly, happy to have done her good deed for the day.

I'm appreciative, though this is a double edged sword. I'm encouraged by the news that my efforts are noticed but dreading my next encounter with Casey. We left things a little sketchy, and in my frustration, I come to find I inadvertently threw him under the bus.

71

Day 29

Day three, no A/C. The boss left at noon yesterday muttering something about a sinus infection. Today, Mike's a no show. I think he's sick of the heat and knows not a lot is going to get done until the situation is remedied.

Several educators lounge in the front office. This lower, inside room is insulated from the heat wave and a good place to dry the sweat from the walk to school.

Mr. Sawyer finds a seat opposing me. "Listen. I wanted to apologize for trouncing your idea the other day." The brow beating from the teachers must've left an impression. "You're new. You don't get how things work, and I could've been kinder."

I run with the olive branch he's extending. "I didn't mean to be disrespectful. The way Mike left the meeting I was very unclear what the expectations were, and he even said, 'divide up how you want.' No one stepped up, and I thought there should be a plan."

"Oh, there's a plan in place," he chortles. "Teachers are *supposed* to get to each of their kids for a block of time."

"That's what I did," I vent, "but then I saw other teachers handing out random work to random students. It's not uniform, and the kids get confused."

"Well, they shouldn't be doing that. They should be seeing their kids." I can tell by the definitiveness of his response that this is a point to contention.

"See, I only heard that just now from you. I've gotten different messages from different teachers." Casey has opened a window into a dysfunction long solidified by the lack of leadership.

"Mike told us last time to see each of our assigned kids," he defends his position.

"Okay," I side with the person I'm trying to ingratiate. "That would've cleared up a lot of my confusion. But still, without a schedule, we had five or six teachers in the same house. Who were with the other two?"

"A glitch in the system." Casey moves us past any sign of squabble or slight with a wispy flick of the hand and light smirk.

"And, no one wants to change it." This revelation is calmly accepted.

"Everyone likes to do their own thing," Casey shrugs. "Mike hasn't told us otherwise."

Day 30

I'm convinced Mike came back today with the sole purpose of chasing us out of the school. After the morning shift yesterday, I came to realize I was one of only three teachers who bothered visiting the houses, and I was not in good company.

"When the cat's away, the mice get lazy," Casey shared his wisdom, chummily, yesterday afternoon. Even I didn't bother to make the rounds for the second half of school. Instead, Ms. Vargas, Casey, and I shared a bag of popcorn from the vending machine and watched an over-the-top action/drama Casey had in his secret stash. Looking up from the movie, I'm drawn to Ms. Vargas' quiet beauty that I determined is derived from a gently caring nature. There is something about a person's face that develops over a lifetime of unassuming, unjudging kindness that can be captivating when discovered. There is nothing physical about her attractiveness, but more of a womblike comfort and warmth she secretes. I just wanted to delicately bask in it regardless of how fleeting.

Today, I time my exit to align with the rat pack as we journey back to the houses. Casey and Julia Vargas are on the younger side, weathered, yet laid back. There is wisdom to be gathered on how to successfully navigate this institution, and I like their model.

Casey imparts some of his understanding as we walk. "I'm surprised you made it in when you did, Jon. That means either you are a relic from a previous budget, or the institution is being proactive."

"I'm a relic." I choose the funnier of the two, knowing full well it could be correct due the 22 month timespan between application and hiring date. Add to that a slow four months of background checks and urine tests, and I might have to call Guinness for the record.

"See that circle of houses down yonder?" Casey motions with his chin, "Those four and the two behind the dietary have been remodeled over the last year for escape and suicide prevention; wouldn't want to harm the little darlings. Before that, we would daily have 300 plus youth come up and the school would be hoppin.

74

That was when we had over 20 teachers," Casey pauses to take a few steps and let it soak in. "You should consider yourself lucky. You get to warm up with three small cottages and acclimate to the increase. I was thrown into the frying pan. Man, we had some good brawls back then." A glazed look indicates I shouldn't interrupt his fond reminiscing. Arriving to Jefferson, bids us farewell.

Two boys who refused to work yesterday are eerily well behaved and hardworking. Franklyn, on the other hand, angrily weaves concentric circles through the dayroom in protest.

He starts sitting to gauge the packet. "This is bullshit! Get outta here so we can have our rec time! You teachers are fucking it up!" Franklyn stands and waves over a guard, "Davis, get him outta here. Let us play cards." He leads the way toward the door to have me follow by swinging his arm to beckon me, "I don't give a shit if I don't get credit. Fuck school!" He knows his efforts are futile and banks down a hallway after a haughty protest of less than a minute. Waving for the guard to follow him, "Put me back in my room until rec."

"While you're taking him, I need Steven Higgins." Intuiting there is no talking Franklyn off the edge, I'll do my best to move on.

"Higgins wouldn't come out for other teachers, but I'll try again." The guards are getting more honest with me. I'm earning their trust and appreciate their expertise as Mr. Higgins is not in the mood for education today either. Both prefer the solitude of their six-by-nines over expanding their minds.

"By the way Jon, if you say that I'm here for the money again, I'll knock your teeth all over the parking lot." Casey has halted our jovial return to the school when an offhand remark strikes a nerve. For as big and tough as I look, I cower from confrontation.

"I was just messing with you. Don't be so touchy; I'm just here to collect a check," I deflect with deprecation to escape the awkwardness.

"Don't get me wrong," he eases as he amends his reaction. "I wouldn't do this for free, but I definitely don't do it for the money." Despite the moment of discomfort, I'm encouraged by Casey Sawyer's passion and purpose. A higher calling, moment of epiphany brought me here, and I take comfort in the fact that my new comrades share my conviction.

"Yes, we are here to change the lives of these downtrodden delinquents." I gaze hopefully into the distance to emphasize my melodramatic point.

This afternoon starts with a picture straight out of the pages of National Geographic: deep in the rainforest, a small wooden boat is floating down a serene yet murky brown river. Suddenly, chum is introduced, and a school of frenetic piranhas froth the water. That's pretty close to the frenzy that happens when a candy bar is presented in a housing unit.

"Masters, that for me?"

"Masters, let me get that."

"Come on Masters, holla at your boy."

Perceiving their pleas are in vain, the groupers disperse, "Man you bogus anyways. I ain't doin no work."

I didn't realize I was so popular. I've never made the acquaintance of any of these young men and couldn't pick their names off of a roster, but they know me.

One familiar fish continues to circle. "Masters, let me get that Snickers up outcha."

"Franklyn, you only did one day of work this week. If you try harder, you might earn achievement of the week."

Recognizing his requests are in vain, he tries to save face, "Fuck you then! I ain't doin your shit!"

The attack happens 12 minutes later. Three students are working quietly when Franklyn sneaks up and tries to grab the Snickers sitting on my thigh. He immediately hides his hand up his sleeve. I think about asking for it back, but this kid moves too quickly. Impulsively grabbing his arm before he's out of reach, I rapidly pat up and down the sleeve.

"Chill, Masters." He shows both hands. "I didn't take it."

I peer down to see the candy bar has slid to the outside of my leg, wedged into the chair. The shame is immediate and hard to disguise. I comfort myself with the thought, *this kid fucks around too much. Now, he knows I'm not to be messed with. Other kids saw this as well and know I'll bite.*

When I was teaching at a therapeutic day school affiliated with a mental hospital, a veteran crisis staff noticed my fumbling greenness. Big Sam pulled me aside one day and shared his wisdom, "Masters, if you're gonna make it here, you got to learn to out-crazy these kids. See, when a kid gets out of pocket, I call him over real close, so as only him and I can hear, and I tell 'em, 'don't make me punch you in the gut, therapeutically.'" Big Sam ended with a wild cackle, and I got a firsthand impression of how the kids viewed him. Time and practice would tell he was dead right.

I chalk the present incident up to a valuable teachable moment for these youth and move on with my group confident that I've made an impression.

Day 32

No power. No prospects. No plan.

After a long week on the cottages, Ms. Peters, Ms. McDonough, and I return to a blacked out school. The teaching staff is informed via word of mouth that the power had been shut off at 2:00. We find out piecemeal that it would be off all day Monday. Mike underhandedly encourages his staff to use a sick day if they wish.

"And waste them when the kids aren't even gonna be here? Nuh uh!" Mrs. Peter's levity speaks to everyone's heart. When working year-round with extremely disturbed individuals (and students), a mental health day can be just what the doctor ordered.

Day 33

I waffle with the idea of calling off but, being new, decide against it. As I drive in, I realize I have no way of reproducing the packet I had lined up for the day. Should've called in.

Ms. Grimly, a sweet African lady from the Bible study I was invited to attend on Tuesdays during lunch, lets me crash in her office in the Clinic. I have a printer and a cool place to hide.

"Mr. Masters, you can come to the lounge and eat lunch with us." Mrs. Peters passes my open classroom door. After beginning my new career with three straight days of lunchtime Bridge, I have hidden in my classroom under the guise of catching up on paperwork to avoid the game (and players) without confronting or offending anyone.

"I generally dislike large groups of people," I disclose. She hoots because I present as a social butterfly to mask a deep-seeded introverted nature. She makes no motion to leave, so I pack up my lunch and follow obediently.

"Mr. Masters, did you hear? Ms. White is retiring." Ms. Peters tends to tell the truth roughly half the time. So, I've learned to be dubious.

"Really? Job security for me. Two teachers will be gone before my first three months are up."

"And, she's getting married!" There's the lie.

"Really! You're kidding. Wait, is she really retiring, Mrs. Wells?"

"She is!" protests Peters with a look of offense. I can't tell if she's really hurt, which adds to the maddening job of deciphering her message.

I choose to go with sarcastically callous. "I need the truth, so I'm ignoring you. The question is directed to you, Mrs. Wells."

"She is retiring," Mrs. Wells reassures in a motherly tone.

"I thought you had to announce two months in advance." My interest is piqued because Ms. White is/was the SPED history teacher, a position I covet. History for me is a fantastic nonfiction storyline that intertwines and repeats over several millennia.

Mrs. Wells continues her lesson, "nope, just two weeks," between bites.

"Why so sudden?" I fain interest, but I really don't care. I have to offer to carry her things to the gate. Not to be cold, but if I have an opportunity to nab a great classroom in the first two months of working here, I'm going to grab it with a Kung Fu death grip. Schools are dog-eat-dog.

"She's getting married!" Peters interjects trying to retrieve the attention.

Peters can be humorous but doesn't know when to let a joke end, "If you want to start a rumor, Peters, tell everyone that Ms. Green wants to trade English to me."

"We don't know she's getting married." Mrs. Wells shares that there is some truth to Peters' shtick. "She's been working it out for a while but didn't want to tell Mike because he might mess with her before she leaves."

"Wow . . . That's incredible," I reply to the short timeframe and the possibly valid perception of my new boss.

"That's reality." Mrs. Wells imposes over her sandwich and down her nose to absorb my eyes. She has enlightened me to the line in the sand and wants confirmation that I'm on the right side.

"Well, on the bright side, that means health, and what else does she teach?" Peters cynically draws the conversation away from politics.

"History is up for grabs." I finish her thought. "That was what I was originally hired for anyway. I'd love to get a crack at it. I have a great unit for Black History Month where I teach *Roots*. I would switch between the book and DVD series for a rounded experience."

"White kids watch out!" Peters bobs her head, pushing herself away from an imagined steering wheel as she pumps the breaks.

"Why do you say that?"

"The black kids will be all riled up lookin for someone to blame."

"You really think so?" I'm a little dejected.

"Yup."

"Mike had the same misgivings when I pitched the idea to him. As teachers, we're supposed to continue to look past the current state of racial tensions by skirting the subject and hoping it changes?" I plead.

"You might be able to succeed with that idea in public school, but here, blood boils quick. I would avoid controversy until you're off probation. It's for your own good." Peters reassuringly touches my forearm, pausing her comedy routine to impart sage advice. If she is my role model, after I'm vested, it's no-holds-barred.

Day 34

The realization that you have firmly planted your foot in your mouth and the ramifications will surely bite you in the ass is an exhilaratingly, yet terrifying, feeling. Adrenaline pumps blood from your neck to your ears; your temples throb. Biology guarantees there is no recovering from what you just said.

Luckily, I get to experience this shoe chewing second hand.

Mrs. Peters banters with a youth I am working with in a silly, argumentative way. She flits her hair about smiling while she explaining to the young man that he would have earned a better grade in her class had he worked as diligently as he is with me currently. When she's had enough of the back and forth, she cuts him off with, "Well, tough stuff!" and blows him a kiss.

Time slows. Each kid registers the shock. I attempt to keep my cheeks from flushing. *Walk away*, I silently will her, *please, walk away*.

"Oh! That was a brain fart. I meant, like, kiss off." *Just walk away!* "I didn't mean to blow you a kiss." Her attempts to cover only reinforce and validate what just transpired.

To the students' credit, or due to shock, they don't respond. It takes a solid 30 seconds before enough blood has drained from our faces to continue working on the lesson. Snickering ensues, but the subject is never broached.

THE A/C IS BACK ON!!! After a grueling eight days without, the hottest of which caused my classroom to register 93 degrees, the compressor roars on at 2:06 PM. Jubilated teachers crank the systems to their max and use fans to circulate the air on the second floor. Nothing brings people closer than triumphing over disaster.

I'm stoked that I get to finally teach in my own space. The librarian, Mr. Frank, compares teaching on the living units to the lion tamers in the circus. "We do best when we're in the room first and the students come in. We have the dominant position. Walking into the houses, you're in their cage. That's when they attack."

I appreciate his analogy after almost two weeks of encounters with boys in shorts, du-rags and flip-flops. Usually, they must wear pants with shirts tucked in at all times for a myriad of safety and etiquette reasons. Normally, youth also wear Velcro sneakers, but security implements an unwritten policy of shower shoes in the house so youth cannot get traction if they want to fight. Most youth are smart enough to flip them off and go at it barefoot. That's why security strictly enforces socks with sandals. Tacky fashion legitimately prevents fights. The relaxed uniform has a calming effect on the youth but can be a hindrance to education.

Capitalizing on the jubilation over central air, I decide to ride the good vibes into Mike's office. "I heard Ms. White is retiring."

"Why yes," Mike's feeling the cool as he lounges away from his desk to give me some attention, "She submitted her paperwork Monday." I can't help but notice the glint in Mike's eye. I think he's sadistically happy she's leaving. We are desperately understaffed, currently having at least half the classrooms empty, and I'd think Mike would welcome a warm body. I won't be critical of his personal biases because the void will require the institute to hire more teachers, and I'll move up the seniority list.

"I was wondering, is anyone in line to take history?" I pry, hat-in-hand.

"Not at the moment." Mike leaves me hanging while relishing my mouse-caught-by-the-tale squirm.

"If it is possible, I'd love to nab it."

"That seems like a possibility." Mike dismisses me cheerily, leaving himself an out.

I go for broke. "Can I pick Ms. White's ear to see what curriculum she has and the progress she's made," I back pedal, "should it become available?"

"I'm afraid that will be difficult." Mike enhances his joy by delivering bad news. "See, she'll be on vacation the next two weeks and is only coming back because the contract requires you to attend your last day. I doubt she'll be much help."

I side step the barrier and leap blindly hoping to find a landing, "Is it possible for me to start teaching history tomorrow?" Mike leans back contemplatively. It's not a 'no,' and I press on. "If I take Ms. White's roster instead of Mrs. McDonough's roster, it's no extra work for you, and I don't have to transfer grades with Mrs. McDonough or interrupt what she has going with her kids. It's a win-win." I smile with reassuring hopefulness that I pray my inner terror doesn't betray. I've way overstepped, and in this uncharted land, there is no telling what Mike will do.

He takes his time with a measured reply. "Why not." I wait for more, and when nothing comes, I bow in gratitude while backing out of the room. Giddily sprinting out of earshot, I won't give him a chance to change his mind.

Day 35

The first day of school has finally arrived. This time it's anticlimactic. After getting to know the kids in small groups during the almost two weeks at the houses, I feel I have a good gauge of my classroom dynamics.

Quotes are meant to inspire people but can leave some baffled. The key is context. I try to inspire a passion for historical relevance within inner-city, mostly minority youth by introducing a quote from *Lies my Teacher Told Me* by James W. Lowen. "Those who don't remember the past are condemned to <u>repeat</u> the 11th grade." I figure I'm a rebel using such a controversial title, and the students will appreciate the repetitive nuances of conquest, revolution, and discrimination throughout history.

Discrimination is the capstone of my presentation because it seems like a go-to complaint for these kids both on the street and while incarcerated. I try to instill in kids who accuse me of being racist that if they cry wolf too many times, people will stop listening, and then when prejudice truly does happen, no one will believe them.

Starting with the Egyptians enslaving and killing Jews, religious persecution evolves to the Romans feeding Christians to the lions and rounds out with the Christians fighting the spread of Islam during the Crusades. The racial discrimination piece of this discussion begins by highlighting how the European "settlers" stole land from and killed the natives. They kidnapped Africans to work the land they stole. During the Civil War, the North needed soldiers, so they exploited freshly arrived Irish immigrants (I shamelessly include my ancestry). To build the transcontinental railroads and fulfill Manifest Destiny, the Chinese were subjugated. And during World War II, Japanese were put into internment camps.

My summation connects Hitler's targeting of the Jews during a German depression to the current targeting of the Hispanic population during a U.S. depression.

I pause for applause as several millennia of interconnection washes over them.

I'm greeted only by blank stares and crickets.

I kybosh the grand, professorial introduction for the last two classes. Instead, I opt to chit-chat to better get to know my students. I should have planned another icebreaker. After almost four weeks out of school, these boys are in no state for the existential tapestry of an idyllic rambler.

Day 37

The great dark cloud of catastrophic storm "Max" has settled upon us. There have been rumors and predictions, but nothing can prepare us for the happening.

For weeks, the state government, local union, and facility management speculated about the closing of the maximum security youth facility. The gossip swirled and blew, but it wasn't until a downspout of students poured onto my class list that the gravity of impending doom struck me. I signed up for a medium-security, cush job. These max kids are going to start a shit-storm.

As a staff, we are impotent to stifle the coming torrent. So, we do the next best thing. "Max kids mean max pay. We better be getting a $120 a month bump," union reps thump their chest in self-righteous indignation.

I can't be too confident that their rage will be quelled considering the governor has already violated the state workers contract for over 12 months, refusing to pay three promised raises adding up to roughly 5-6%, and forcing the union into a deluge of litigation.

The icing on the cake: "These kids are all being paroled in 60 days or less. So, that means they aren't max anymore." The administration definitively illustrates the futility of fighting them. Just bend over; they know where to stick it.

The weatherman always overdoes it. He thrives on the fear of the impending. The max kids are quite pleasant. All choose seats in the front row. All engage in appropriate conversations with me and their peers. All complete assigned work diligently. Overall, the classes are pleasantly well behaved. Because the current youth have heard thundering for weeks, they are ineffectually in awe when the tempest of these mythological max kids arrive, and overall behavior is greatly improved.

I may have spoken prematurely. During fourth period, "Crazy Clown Love," is drizzled over every surface this red-headed albino can find (desk, notebook, folder, ID, & eraser). I think he must've chosen this particular gang because he can save money on the face paint.

Prior to this display of artwork, he made his first impression trying to steal a notepad by shoving it down his pants, leaving a visible outline protruding above his belly button, and claiming I didn't give him one. He inexplicably found it on the floor when I threatened him with a body search.

Day 39

I am blessed to experience my first prison fight today. It happens between 4th and 5th blocks. Two kids leave line movement to settle their differences closer to the wall. It is considerate that they don't want to delay the other students from attending their classes. I've had over five years of physical intervention experience and training, but this is a foreign environment, and these kids can throw serious heat. It resembles a hockey melee, grabbing each other's shirt and blasting as hard as they can. Students huddle in a tight semi-circle and run from down the hall to get a better view. For me to respond, I'd have to push through an unfamiliar mob to try to separate two unidentified, wild-eyed young men. As I acclimate to this environment, I don't feel scared necessarily, but I also don't throw myself in harm's way. Back to the wall is the safest place to be.

As one youth puts the other in a headlock, a single responding staff radios for help but doesn't attempt to intervene. With the walky-talky squawk, the mob loosens, and some youth begin to fade down the hall while keeping an interested eye on the action until the end. Two more guards come bounding through the back staircase. The jangling of keys cues the aggressor, and he relinquishes his dominant position to face the wall with his hands behind his head. The other youth mirrors him, so the two who were just brawling are now an arm's length apart posing for surrender. The forty plus onlookers disperse in a matter of seconds not wanting to be identified or associated with the outcome.

As the potential terror of the situation drains, I can't help but wonder, *what stopped the mob in the hall from tearing apart the school and attacking the staff?* Every youth seems to understand the procedures and consequences and has a healthy fear of both. This validates the structure and discipline I left my last school to pursue. The ominous presence of "the institution" is felt even during a period of havoc.

Day 40

When nature calls . . .

It is awkward, at best, to utterly uncomfortable to have to use the bathroom any time during the three hour chunks students are in the school.

Scenario 1: I could ask hall security to watch my class while I go. Security doesn't appreciate environments they don't control, which is understandable, and the classroom is the teacher's domain. The transition of staff and change of expectations inevitably sets the students up to test boundaries, get loud, and stop working. It's hard enough to get them to work for me. They're definitely not working for a non-teacher.

Scenario 2: Hold it. I drink well over a gallon of water a day. The white-hot, bend-over pain that my kidneys articulate as they try to push out the front, back, and bottom of me eliminates this as an option.

Scenario 3: Use the classroom washroom.

Plus side, it has a window, so I can keep an eye on the students. If timed right, the students will continue working uninterrupted.

Minus, it has a window! At any point, a student can run up for a peek. Not an easy conversation or situation to traverse.

Also, my hands are tied if a student runs and jumps over my desk to steal candy or supplies or damage the projector. In this case, a choice would have to be made. I could A) try to pinch, zip, and run after the offender, all without pissing myself, or B) own it. Act as if it was all part of my omnipresent plan as "Teacher." Don't let on that I'm bothered by the invasion. I was testing them, someone failed, and I'll send them out with a casual referral. Stay stoic.

Life's about the adventure.

The great philosophical debate, "to pee or not to pee," allows class change to sneak up on me. In the midst of the helter-skelter, a note is discretely placed on my desk. I only become aware of its existence after the lesson has begun.

Opening the thrice folded parchment, I'm introduced to a giant, phallic superhero. "Jamie the Super Dick" is inscribed at the base (balls) of the illustration. It seems artfully crafted and anatomically correct save the added arms, legs, and face (including sunglasses).

Embarrassingly unaware of who might have bestowed me such homage, I discretely slide the drawing under a textbook before it causes a stir. As I check the previous period's roster, I can't detect any youth who would have reason for such a bold slight. Scanning the present audience, I narrow it down to two possible suspects and settle in for patient observation until the culprit slips up.

I don't wait long. "Mr. Masters, did you get my note?" A quietly studious, relatively new student catches me off guard. Never having said neigh to me, Sampson didn't blip my radar as the culprit.

His confession is thin and could be circumstantial if he changes his story later, so I attempt to set the hook, "What note? Is there something you need?"

Sampson takes the bate. "Nah, I drew a superhero in Mrs. McDonough's class and wanted you to have it."

"Thanks for the admission." I smile triumphantly as I remove a disciplinary ticket from my desk, "I had no idea who wrote that, and you would have been the last person I expected."

His previously snarky confidence betrays him. Sampson tries to defend his flagrant faux pas, "What, you can't take a joke?" His grin wavers tentatively.

"Mr. Sampson," I explain, "there'll never be a time when drawing a giant penis with a cape is an appropriate student/teacher interaction. What were you thinking?"

"I thought it was funny." He tries to laugh it off. "I thought you were cool and would appreciate it."

Some students 'honeymoon' longer than others. Being in a new environment allows them to put a fresh foot forward, and I'll be the last to burst such attempts at a noble beginning. Up until this moment, Sampson appeared to be heading down the right path. "Whether I'm 'cool' or not, this is wildly inappropriate." Little did I know that this young man is desperately lost in the woods.

"So you're writing me a ticket?" Sampson is hurt and confused by my reaction. He legitimately perceived that three days of attendance have fostered a bond close enough for such a crude attempt at humor.

"You've left me no choice." I try to soften my approach to his apparent social deficit, "As long as there are no further issues, you can stay and complete your work. But, I have to document this."

"Fuck that!" Sampson's true colors shine through, "Just cuz your pussy ass can't fuckin take a joke doesn't mean I have to take a hit." Throwing his pencil from the back row off the blackboard, Sampson clears his desk of folder and textbook with one sweep and storms out of class, slamming the door.

Prior to lunch, as I attempt to recount such a bizarre story, I can't help but laugh. Most mental health professionals would say my response doesn't fit the gravity of the situation, but I find humor is the healthiest way to cope. To delve into the depraved experience that led this young man to such a juncture only serves as a haunting weight to be shouldered.

Mr. Vincennes, juvenile supervisor I previously connected with on the softball field, is not amused. He presents as regimented and disciplined and expects the youth to carry themselves similarly. Trying to explain the missing building blocks that lead to the kid's skill deficits is not acceptable to Vincennes. His approach garnishes a certain amount of success, so most staff don't interrupt his line of thinking.

Vincennes assures me he'll have a talk with Sampson, and I'm left guiltily debating if his is the most effective approach for such a disturbed youth man.

Day 41

Sleepers! They drive me nuts. What is the most disrespectful action a student can possibly exhibit in a classroom? Sleep!

Sleep speaks, "You're boring." "You're IrReLeVeNt!" "I DON'T CARE!!!"

In regular ed., sleeping is unheard of. The teacher needs to reach each and every student in the classroom. If a student is sleeping, the teacher is not effectively educating.

During my stint at a mental health facility, I had sleepers. I instructed those who couldn't keep their heads up to stand or visit the hall staff. I was pulled aside quickly. "Jon, are you sending kids out for sleeping?" my former principal inquired.

"Yeah. Why?" I asked innocently.

"Jon, we have bigger problems to deal with," he educated me; "It's a waste of time to piss off tired kids. Just leave them be."

"But, I can't let kids sleep in my class. If sleeping becomes acceptable, it will become contagious," I protested not understanding there was any other way. These kids were already lost; would we allow them to slip further?

Though not known for his compassion, the principal softly broadened my scope. "You have to figure out a way to handle this in class. You need to manage as much as you can before you send kids out. Sleeping is simply not disruptive. Teach around it."

One of my favorite grad school professors did a memorable lecture on "students' rights." He implored the future educators of America that every student has the "right to succeed," and it's our job to equip them with all the tools they'll need. At the other pole, he explained, "students have a right to fail." If we as teachers do everything in our power and give each student a plethora of opportunities to succeed, those students may still choose failure. Educators need to let students make that choice because failure teaches as much if not more than success. Hopefully a kid will ask himself, *Did I just waste four months of my life with nothing to show for it?* The answer and subsequent life choices can change a life forever.

My principal further enhanced my behavior management approach, "Jon, these kids are not normal (huge surprise). They can't just listen and follow a directive because mommy or daddy or teacher said so. When adults make a decision, they evaluate the choices. Each choice has consequences, both positive and negative. Responsible adults choose the best option for them personally and, if they're really considerate, for the whole of the group. We need to give these kids choices and help them understand the consequences, and sometimes, we need to let them fall flat on their face to learn from the bumps."

Unable to assimilate this new idea to my teaching schema, I inquire, "So, how should I handle my sleepers?"

"As they are nodding off or prepping to sleep, inform them that they should be doing work. If they choose not to, they'll have to make up the work or take it home to turn in for late credit. If they choose to ignore the make-up work, their grade will suffer. And if they don't pass their classes, they have to spend more time with your happy ass." He pauses to smirk at his gibe. "I think they'll comply eventually."

"Thanks," I retort, disingenuously, knowing I have either been ribbed or insulted.

Allowing snoozers to slumber worked well at the mental health facility. I wouldn't let students get too comfortable (no lying on sweatshirts or on the floor, though they tried), but I allowed them to sleep. This approach motivated me to give out grade sheets every Friday. The students could track their grade progress, up or down, and I could connect it to their attentiveness. I'd done everything I could. The students had the tools for achievement. Success or failure was a choice, but it wasn't mine.

At the next alternative school, they prescribed to the "poke the bear" model. We had to define the behavior the student was exhibiting, explain the expectation, and if the student couldn't acquiesce, he/she was given a penalty. Three penalties = one behavior referral. The problem: this meant I had to wake up a student three times and then a fourth to send him/her out.

94

This wasn't a popular practice because a student went from making no noise to creating a lot of noise (and sometimes irreparable damage).

The matter was ultimately settled using Erickson's model for hierarchical needs. It stated that students couldn't learn while exhausted. We concluded it was best to let them rest and kick it in the butt later. Referrals were still written but processed when the student was bright eyed.

I've learned to appreciate the snore over the roar.

Inside Boys Home, they don't let students sleep through class. The SBS behavior expectation that is plastered in every classroom and littered throughout the hallways is that youth come "Prepared to Learn." If they don't, they receive Time Out Tickets, and a trip to Ms. Wells helps them pinpoint why they aren't ready.

Since this is my fourth go-around, I won't be waking them up. The first time, I'll give them a pass. Everyone can have a bad day once in a while. The second time merits a referral, but I don't have to wake them up. That is a negative association that, frankly, I don't want in this cage. I'll leave the rousting to the Youth Correction Officer.

It's an evolutionary fact: everybody tries to pass the buck on being the bad guy. When it's my turn to do the dirty work, I'll own it. But, that doesn't mean I run to the front of the line every time.

Last week, I completely forgot because of the extended summer intermission, but this week, I write it on the board to highlight my zeal. It's "High-Five Friday!" While at the psychiatric facility, I ran into a misunderstood young man who walked up to any and every female staff attempting to sell them on the idea of "Free Hug Thursday." Seeing as he had no takers and trying to relieve some awkward tensions, I offered to give this young man a side-hug to teach appropriate boundaries.

"Free Hug Thursday" caught on quickly paving the way for "High Five Friday." At the end of the week, we tall, athletic, young men would run toward each other, jump as high as we could, and slap hands in the middle of the hallway. It's a tradition I carried to my last school (less jumping but more participation), and I'm not about to let the flame die now.

The boys cautiously embrace the novelty as I stand in the doorway, open palm raised. Most participate with muted energy. Only two students out of my four classes decline to participate. We're just getting started; they'll come around.

Day 42

My vast recollective knowledge of the abstract and useless comes in handy when making connections to lessons. The only other place it remotely applies: yelling at game show contestants.

The class has navigated the Bering Strait theory of early Native Americans, and now we skip forward several thousand years to detail the groupings in more depth. While discussing the Inca's, we find one of their great accomplishments is the building of roads to connect the vast empire. This made it easier for runners to carry news great distances (with handoffs, periodically) and for people and supplies to travel.

To make such a monumental accomplishment relevant for nodding-off, easily uninterested adolescents, I explain how the Roman Empire did the same to connect and rule most of Europe, the Middle East, and Northeast Africa. I pose a question to pique interest and promote participation. "How has America connected their vast empire?"

The huddled masses stir. "Roads," offers a youth named Jackson.

"What kind?" I push.

"Highways." Franklyn interjects.

"What about before cars?" This pushes them beyond the stone ages. *Was the earth inhabited before the automobile?*

"Railroads," a mousey white kid in the front row answers confidently.

"Yes, Mr. Thompson. The U.S. had a strong core belief in the middle 1800s. It was called Manifest Destiny, and it meant it was God's divine plan for America to connect the Atlantic and Pacific oceans. And we used railroads to do it before interstates. Did you know that when building the interstates, for every seven miles of highway, architects planned one mile of straight road without any bridges or curves? Now why do you think that is?"

Every kid is eating out of my hand. They will not be able to leave the classroom without knowing this answer. "It was designed so a plane could land during an emergency or wartime. Do you know where America probably got that idea from?" I leave just enough space to draw these kids to the edge of their seats, "Hitler." The kids can't look away as I doodle on the board while illustrating my point. "After World War I, the Germans needed jobs and money because of a depression caused by their losing the war. Hitler rallied German pride and loyalty by building up a superhighway called the Audubon. Has anyone heard of it?"

"Yeah, that's where they race Lamborghinis!" an enthused Jackson answers.

"I don't know about races, but the Audubon is such a finely built highway that many parts of it have no speed restrictions, and people do take their high-end cars there to test the limits. Does anyone know what this symbol is?" I've finished drawing a quartered circled that I have shaded two diagonal sections white.

"That's BMW!" Franklyn confidently chimes.

"Correct. Do you know where this symbol originated?" The youth have been transformed. The 'I don't give a shit' attitude and bravado has been suppressed, and a child-like wonderment is climbing to the surface. The developmental stages these kids missed by having to grow up on the mean streets are untethered to shine through, if only for a moment. "There is a popular belief that the white symbolizes the moving propellers of a plane and the blue is the sky in the background. After World War I, Germany had sanctions that prevented them from building up an air force. BMW made cars, but they were also used as a cover for Hitler building his planes."

The awe created from this winding tangent has given me priceless credibility. As the lesson flashes back to Central and South American tribes, participation is at an all-time high.

As the lesson draws to a close, Franklyn, who had declined to complete any work yesterday, pauses during his exit to turn and say, "Mr. Masters, you really taught me something today."

This simple statement validates all the patient foundational work I've done with him. I have to hang on to this moment. Gems like this are few and far between. Dusting them off will help get me through the hard days ahead.

Day 43

"I'll whoop yo ass, Masters!"

"Bring it! I'm sittin right here!"

"You don't want to fuck with me," the young man says, losing confidence and puzzled by my response.

"Let's dance. All that extended time you be getting, I'll get a couple months' vacation. Let's see what's up."

Silence.

My first period of the day gets roaring with an impulsive outburst. Mr. Franklyn, my star of the previous day, returned to a state of participation refusal. He's upset because I called him to task for passing by the classroom without entering, and now, I've given him the ultimatum to sit quietly and complete his assignment, or he'll lose his points. (Ms. Peters just explained this whole losing points thing to me, and apparently, it's a big deal.)

I smile to break the tension. "Franklyn, this is not a situation where you need to hulk up. You gotta choose those times better, and they need to be very few and far between. I'm not talkin about your girl or your momma. I'm not threatening you. I'm asking you to work quietly in class. It's not that big a deal."

With a crooked smile, Franklyn accepts my good intentions. "I got you, Mr. Masters."

Day 44 On Monday, one max student in fourth block and one max student in fifth block cleverly used hair to represent their gangs. First, my "Wicked Clown" looked even funnier with a full muttonchop sideburn on the right side of his face. Upon closer inspection, I noticed he didn't have a match on the left. I was impelled to ask. Answer: "Hair doesn't grow there." Perfectly normal.

During fifth block, a student who had walked in with a full mop of hair the previous day came in with a clean dome except for an inch strip at last inch of the nape of his neck which still had eight inches of flowing hair. The length of this hairstyle brags about the amount of time a person has been in a certain gang. Said gang member shaves his head clean, then subsequent buzz cuts allow only

99

base of the skull to lengthen. Over time, it grows from nothing to show the length of commitment. It can make quite a statement when done correctly. This kid cheated.

Even more bothersome than his half-baked pledge to the gang is the fact that this haircut happened in prison. Either he did it himself, at which point a Youth Correctional Officer should've said, "you missed a spot," and sent him back to his room. Or, our barbers did it, at which point a YCO should've said, "hey, you missed a spot," and had the barber finish the job.

By fifth period, this youth had passed at least 60 inmates and 20 staff. Why I had to write the incident report escapes me.

Evidently my shaggy friend got a talking to. Today, he thanks me for noticing his style by tagging his book and a one-by-two-foot spot on the blackboard. More paperwork for me and his hair remains unaltered.

Lesson learned: snitches get stitches.

Day 45

Very purposefully, I'm sure, Strategic Behavior System's meetings are scheduled for Thursday mornings. Hump day is a grind for staff and students alike. The kiddies have acclimated enough to their surroundings that Wednesdays are full of experimentation with repercussion. To be put in a state prison, a youth has to have appeared before a judge enough times for the judge to have attempted several softer approaches, which the youth has bucked. Finally, the exasperated judge has no other resort. That or they have done something truly heinous. In either case, their moral barometer is broken, and any subtle impulse is usually acted upon. After surviving the horrors of hump-day, a little morning break relieves the burdens of many. For those not assigned to the meeting, the morning is an opportunity for solitary refreshment.

We few, we proud, we behavior reformers enjoy the same respite from the youth while lofting idyllic scenarios around on how to improve the school and facility. Or, at least, that's how it's supposed to go. Following my second meeting, Mr. Sawyer fed me a friendly tidbit that new teachers are invited to SBS meetings as a dog and pony show. Those who bark will be penalized.

It's a shame too because I had made a nice acquaintance with Dr. French, and we directed the previous conversation on the importance of semantics when delivering therapeutic principals in a behaviorist environment. Language must always be converted to the positive. Security volleyed examples that we returned with subtle tweaks that truly do make all the difference. I think Dr. French took a liking to me, like most mental health professionals, because I tend to focus on reforming our wards' actions over their need for formal education. After all, the kids aren't here for bad grades.

I make it my business to befriend counselors, social workers, and therapists because they've helped me survive the moral scarring of the clinical environment. Any person newly enmeshed in an inescapable madhouse goes through a progression of emotions. First comes terror. When the door clicks, whether deadbolt or magnetically held, the mortal question of "am I going to make it out alive?" inevitably crosses the mind. As the terror fades, replaced by burgeoning confidence, the true depravity of these kids' situations comes to rest in your chest, threatening to crush it. Alcohol abuse is rampant, and some personnel are prescribed psychotropics. Everyone needs a release from the overtly apparent evil of this world. I lean on the wisdom, training, and sofas of mental health professionals to find balance and free therapy.

Dr. French is not in attendance today. In his stead is the chief of security. This tall, fat, widow's peaked ginger has a kind of smug mug that makes me want to punch him right in that paunch he wears so proudly, just to see the "Oh!" on his face as this windbag deflates. I surmise he's been called to attend by Mike to lessen the tangential impact security makes. Given an open forum to express their opinions, security is more than happy to explain why every nook and cranny of this place is creaky. I enjoy the verbal sparring because it challenges me to explain and justify the system we're implementing. Mr. Hicks and Ms. Brown clearly view security as subordinates but have no power to rebuff them. So, they've called in the chief for more clout. We all have been inaudibly encouraged to sit quietly and bobble our heads politely.

This being my third meeting, a pattern has emerged. Casey Sawyer is the moderator, but he cautiously takes his cues from Mike and Lashonda Brown. Casey explained that Lashonda was in charge of SBS until she thought she was getting a promotion to another facility. Rumor has it that Mike blocked the advancement because he is useless and lazy, and dangling positions over Lashonda got her to do all his work. He couldn't part with his prize pony. Lashonda can't take her hand off the throat of anything she does or has micromanaged. So, to keep the peace, Casey gives her and Mike the lead.

Character education is a hot topic. We're supposed to teach a different trait every Tuesday during second period. The consistency is hit or miss, with most of the education staff wide of the target. During my portion of character ed., I foster a five to ten minute discussion introduced by a question for which the boys need jot down a short answer. This way, they engage their minds before they open their mouths. For the second time in three weeks, Ms. Brown asks Ms. Wells to present her new lesson on empathy, and Ms. Wells is again unprepared, saying, "I'm putting on the finishing touches. I'll have it in teachers' mailboxes by Tuesday morning." Never in my professional life have I seen it so acceptable to fall short of expectations. At least it makes me look good.

Ms. Wells steers the attention off her by sharing the latest round of Time Out Tickets. The TOTs have been on the rise with the heat. Ms. Brown chalks it up to the reintroduction of school after summer break and the kids desire to be running the streets right now. No one objects.

We putter around a couple of other bullet points, and the meeting ends early. SBS is largely an academic initiative, in that it isn't implemented or enforced in any other area of our campus. Without any new faces in attendance for training purposes, these interdisciplinary meetings are mainly used to share what's happening in the school and to utilize other departments to further the academic effort. The Boys Home mission statement proudly claims that education reduces recidivism. From what I've seen, our academia isn't contributing either way. The kids who enter and leave with the tools to succeed, hopefully will. If the school is at the top of its game, we're not impeding the youth already on the right path. Needless to say, every non-educator is beleaguered to be chosen for such a myopic effort as SBS.

In the recession of the meeting, Mike asks me to accompany him to his office.

"Close the door and have a seat." A closed-door meeting gives me a pit in my stomach, but I reassure myself with the fact that I didn't say a thing during the meeting. "Jon, some disturbing things about you have been brought to my attention. Firstly," blindsided, the blood evacuates my face as I try to reference anything I could have said or done that led to this moment. During my six years of teaching, I've never had a conversation start like this, "one of the youth shared with me that you and your wife are 'trying' to have a baby all the time. He even said you illustrated the point with a thrust," (Mike reenacts his description for effect).

"I assure you I said nothing like that. I let the kids play 20 questions to get to know me. They asked if I had kids, and I told them my wife and I **hadn't** started trying yet."

"Uh-huh," Mike's speculative gaze makes me believe that he is leaning toward trusting the story of the incarcerated. "This young man also said you were making racist statements."

Mike leaves this hang to gauge my reaction. Evidently being young, tall, and Arian gets a racist stamp firmly imprinted on my forehead. I know the harder I rub, the redder my face will get and the guiltier I look. I've weathered this accusation before, sadly, and have found the only way to withstand this storm is to casually deny, not get offended, and walk on eggshells for a couple weeks. Things will blow over until the next accusation, and the dance begins again.

"Jon, you need to choose your words more carefully around here." By the way Mike levels these words at me, I'm certain protesting is not in my best interest.

I leave the office steamrolled and dejected. If this was just a case of mistaken phraseology, I think I could bounce back. But, the way Mike wholeheartedly sided with the incarcerated before even hearing a defense makes me feel like a boy who's just been given a whooping by his father. The scariest thing is I'm unclear what I can change to avoid the same result. I will live in the constant fear of Mike taking off his belt, and I think he likes it that way.

Shaking, I'm so livid, I trounce back to my classroom. Since I can't stand up to Mike, I decide to kick the dog. I visualize how I'd address the youth who defamed me should I have the opportunity and the courage. A negative train races though my head to release the steam from unrelievable outrage:

Racist!? You want to call me RACIST!? You ignorant son of a bitch!!! YOU, sitting there telling everyone you're gonna be the next Tony Montana, with your "I don't give a fuck" attitude, telling me how much money you make "on the street," wanna call me racist.

NO, you stupid fuck. I'm not a racist; I'm a teacher. I get paid to push you. You can't take it because every time you bitch for more than 30 seconds your mommy gives you everything your heart desires.

You know you're right. I do discriminate. I discriminate against every wanna be, hip-hop banger, who can't read much less tie his shoes, and thinks just because he can afford a RocaWear ensemble (that's an outfit, stupid) he's going to be a future millionaire. The

104

reason rappers with no education are rich and famous is because they're the exception to the rule. You ain't nothin special!

Do me a favor. If you think you don't need this school thing, when you wake up, take a long, hard look in the mirror. Repeat after me, "I don't know shit; I don't KNOW shit, I DON'T KNOW SHIT!" Go to the kitchen, eat a heaping bowl of humility for breakfast, and go sweat your ass off at some minimum wage, go-nowhere-in-a-HURRY job for 12 hours a day. When you get home and you're too tired to lift a fork to your mouth, that's when practice for the rap battle or NBA career begins. Good Luck!

Even if you can pull it off, and you happen to be the 1 in 1,000,000 lucky bastard to get a rap deal, you still need an education, dipshit. You're going to be 20 something with a couple of million dollars. No more income + no skills + no common sense = broke by 30 and back to sweatin. That's if you don't kill yourself first.

Day 48

A soapbox flyer and two union representatives greet me as I walk through the first deadbolt door of the front gate. One hands me the pamphlet as the other explains, "Here is the latest information on our suit against the state. It is in your best interest to contact your legislative representatives and tell them you want your back pay."

They wish me farewell with sinister smiles that give me the impression they only care about forwarding an agenda. The smile is menacing enough to make me think their suggestion was more like an order. *Will they know if I've contacted my state rep?* Falsely reassuring myself that they can't possibly find out while secretly developing a conspiracy theory, I collect my keys and head to school.

From my minimal experience thus far, the union's sole purpose is to race every slight that occurs inside the institution into the administrative offices and jam it down "management's" throat. This leads to very hostile relations. Management is constantly covering their butts, and union officials are pressuring the line staff to file a grievance over every change in wind direction.

The union should be a mediator between administration and the people, giving us protection and a voice. Instead, the line staff is stuck in the middle as the union lobs grenades and management figures out how to contractually stick it to the laymen. A little civility would go a long way on both sides. But, by the looks of it, this Hatfield and McCoy battleground has long been entrenched. I'll do my best to navigate the no man's land while presenting niceties to both sides.

Besides, this contractual issue predates me by over a year. I've been informed that my salary is based on an old schedule, and by the looks of things, I could stand to get an immediate $3900 raise if the union wins. So, I settle on the fact that I signed the dotted line and didn't dispute the offer. If I get the raise and back pay, bully for me. If not, oh well.

Nature calls halfway through second period. I've made peace with a protocol of assigning the students an independent task and tiptoeing to take the quickest pee of my life. I keep the light inside the bathroom off to give me more privacy and to prevent the boys from knowing I am watching them while I urinate. No problems so far.

Today, the door should post a biohazard sign for the amount of toxic dumping going on. When I inquire why the third youth is so adamant about sitting in a putrid box, I'm educated by another. "His bunky has him shitblocked."

"*Bunky*? Has him *shitblocked*?" there are at least two words I must add to my lexicon.

"Yeah, Mr. Masters, you've seen our cracker-box rooms. If you take a shit, you have to sit in it for two or three hours. Some bunkmates don't appreciate having to smell another man's ass for so long, so they don't allow their bunky to shit in the room."

Bewildered, "Can't you complain to security?" I can't wrap my head around the situation.

"You're tellin me that you'd have the balls to snitch to staff that you're being shitblocked? Most guys are too embarrassed. Most of us try to dump in school or when we go see our counselor. If you time it right, you can shit just when we're being let out for rec or dietary, and when you come back, the room's cleared."

Enlightening.

I motion for the security staff on the corner to come watch my class so I can use the teacher's facilities. He's not readily willing but perks up when I offer him chocolate.

As I leave, the guard greets the class, "OH MY GOD, BOYS! It smells like gay sex in this bitch!"

A youth mistakenly tries to trap the guard, "Winston, how do you know what gay sex smells like?"

"Well, it reeks of sex in here, and all I see is dudes." I cover my mouth to muffle the sudden gurgle and hang around just long enough to see each young man's head fall, ashamed. You'd think they wouldn't be this easily embarrassed when they're overeager to discuss every detail of the frequency, duration, and motivation of each ejaculation inside their rooms, as if they've conquested the female staff of their fantasies. I guess, deep down, they're just scared little boys.

Day 51

Once again, I'm greeted by a "no school" sign in the education office. I could really get used to random days off, especially on Fridays.

Mike beats me to, "High Five Friday!" as he overzealously yet awkwardly offers me a raised palm in an attempt to join the new craze. Apparently, he's gotten past the fact that I'm a sex-crazed maniac who gets off by sharing my bedroom mischief with underage boys. "Jon, step into my office. I've got your balls."

Stunned by a phrase that should never exit a supervisor's lips, regardless of how much he believes it to be true, I tentatively follow. Mike holds up a bag containing a deflated blue physioball. The blood recirculates to my face as he makes several crude jokes about his wife leaving him unfulfilled. A week ago, I was admonished for being a pervert, but now I'm just one of the boys.

Mike hands me an all plastic, accordion-style foot pump and gives me a ball to inflate. Mike explains how blessed I am because he ordered the foot pump special, "to make things easier." The device proves as futile as it looks, so I resort to using the hand pump that came with the set. Even Ms. Erikson, Mike's office assistant, joins the fun by making note of the repetitive motion as I steady the ball between my knees. I can't help but blush at a self-pleasure pun delivered by a woman older than my grandmother.

At the tail end of a ten minute pumping session that has left me with a sweat-soaked shirt and numb forearms, Mike passes along some information while he figures I'm too winded to protest. "By the way Jon, you will need to report to Southern State Penitentiary for Correctional Orientation Training on Monday. C-O-T is a security crash course they give to employees who don't attend the five week academy training for security guards in the capitol. It will help you understand the ins and outs of handling various crisis situations inside the institution."

I tremble to think that I've been working here almost two-and-a-half months underequipped, "Shouldn't I have taken that before I started?"

"Ideally, yes. But, scheduling is a nightmare with all the different facilities and staff start dates. We shoot to get you there within your first six months." Mike glibly adds to my ever lengthening mental list of things that 'should be done' to keep staff and wards safe.

My only comfort is Mr. Vincennes's repetitive explanation to my operational questioning, "Common sense is not so common here at the state."

"Isn't that the place with the 30 foot cement walls?" I appeal, cautiously impressing that I didn't sign up for that.

"Yeah, they are 30 feet into the ground too, so no one can dig themselves out. You'll be in the processing center, outside the wall." I exhale in relief. "Mr. Sawyer was the last one to go. He can give you directions on how to get there. Be there at eight sharp. Training will last four days, so I will see you next Friday."

Taking my cue to leave, I exit with a ball under each arm, turning sideways to navigate the doorway.

"What in the hell is that?" Casey can't help but laugh at the feebleness of my stature as I ask him for directions to Southern Penitentiary while balancing giant balls against my hips. "You've got to be kidding me. Mike wants you to teach with the kids sitting on those? It's going to be non-stop dodgeball if the boys don't bounce through the ceiling first."

Looking forlorn, "I share that sentiment, but what am I supposed to do?"

"Definitely tell Mike you can't do it," he lounges and laughs.

"I can't disappoint the boss," I dejectedly entreat. "I'm too new."

"Then you, my friend, have yourself a conundrum." Casey sadistically enjoys this way too much while, at the same time, he empathizes with a plight from his recent past.

"So, how do I get to South Pen?"

"You're gonna want to write this down." He cracks himself up. "Just kidding." He wipes away a fake tear. "Look it up online. The big thing is that you have to turn down the side street next to it and go to the back, not the front entrance. You'll think you're going too far to reach the parking lot you need to turn into, but don't turn in too soon. Mrs. McDonough did that, and a guard in the tower yelled at her to turn around while pointing an assault rifle at her windshield."

"Really?"

"Yeah," he chuckles. "Ask her about it when she gets back from Janesville. Retelling the story gets her feathers all ruffled." Casey continues his gayety as I kick the balls towards my classroom.

I double back to ask if he can help me carry a table into my room to see how the physioballs will fit in my seating arrangement.

As I sit on one to get the lay of the land, and the desk comes up to the armpits of my well over six foot frame, Casey can't help himself. "Sorry dude, your balls are too small."

My parade back to Mike's office, balls in hand, (I should have just brought one to illustrate my point) includes a mad scramble as to how to disappoint him in the softest possible way. I've come to understand the process for the acquisition of funds is intentionally so burdensome that few even attempt it. Add this to Mike's propensity for lethargy, and I'm in a great position to be killed as the messenger.

I knock gingerly, "Mike, I think we have a problem."

He waves me in and sits back in his chair, arms crossed, eyeing me expectantly.

"Well, Mr. Sawyer helped me bring a desk into my room, and upon sitting on the ball next to the desk, we realized it will be cumbersome for academics. See for yourself," I role a ball around for him to sit on next to his desk. He would have to stretch his neck to rest his chin on the surface.

"About how many inches do you need to take off each desk?" He can't be serious. Mike's answer to our height problem is not to return and exchange; it's to cut each desk down.

"At least six inches." I'm tempted to move a stack of papers to reestablish eye contact.

Mike ponders my assessment as he stares dead-on at the pile. A passing teacher breaks his concentration, "Gary, can you come in here?"

A lanky, 60-something gentleman with a tan soaked in for years to the point of wrinkles saunters in the door. I've been acquainted with our woodshop teacher, Mr. Park, through the Tuesday lunchtime Bible study he leads in one of the classrooms. He's a carpenter, a free-spirit, and he dons a salt 'n pepper beard with a matching white ponytail, "What's up?"

"Gary, I will need you to coordinate with Mr. Masters to cut down some tables for his classroom." Napoleon orders from behind a barricade.

"No problem, Jon. Just let me know what you need." Mr. Park strolls away as if his gait was never interrupted. I marvel at the level of distain the teachers have for our principal. I haven't had the seasoning to fully assess Mike, but Gary Park has made his peace by resolving to help me while completely ignoring Mike.

I excuse myself. "I'll coordinate with Mr. Park, if need be. Let's hold off until I get back to see if there's another solution."

"Keep me apprized." Mike settles back into his booster seat and bestows me with an apparent no-win burden.

Training Week

To leave enough time to get to Southern State Penitentiary, I set my alarm 45 minutes early on Sunday night. The traffic pattern makes the drive to South Pen between a 35 and a 90 minute commute. I aim for 75 minutes to be safe and arrive at just past 7:30.

I don't want to seem overzealous, so I wait in my car until quarter of and mosey up to what appears to be their 'front gate.' Entering an alcove that would be uncomfortable for two people, I survey a familiar looking entry to my right and a stack of twenty 12 by 12 lockers with orange keys similar to what you would find at a bus station. I note that this would be a nice addition to our alcove, so valuables don't have to be left in our cars to withstand the elements.

A female guard on the other side of a Plexiglas window disrupts my musing, "State your business."

"Sorry," I answer bewilderedly, "I'm here for training; C-O-T training."

"ID," the guard instructs, and I slide it through the indented half-cylinder passage beneath the Plexiglas barrier. She turns to her partner as she glances at my driver's license, "Mack, is there a training today?"

Her partner checks a clipboard, "Not on the master schedule," he offers.

"Please wait there a second," the female guard instructs me as if I have any other option. She makes a fruitless call, then leaves the office. The door to my right clicks, and my new friend beckons me in. "Who sent you here?"

"I came from Boys Home." I leave my answer succinct, unsure if I have done something wrong or am being interrogated.

"Weird. Larry, can you pat this gentleman down, and we'll see if we can get to the bottom of this." Pat downs have become routine. Being new, I'm targeted by the security at our facility for 'random' morning searches. As I get to know the guards, familiarity makes the intimate proximity quite uncomfortable, and I've noticed the frequency of the searches has decreased.

112

"Follow me." My new acquaintance leads the way down a zigzagging corridor that offers a view of a small enclosed courtyard connected to a lunchroom. As we proceed further, the guard uses her ring of keys to lead me into a cubicle maze with private offices on the periphery. She ducks into a small office to inquire, "Dr. Brunswick, do we have C-O-T training here today?"

"Why yes, Sheila," the doctor shares melodically, "It will be in the classroom of annex G. I believe it starts at nine."

An apparent realization washes over Sheila. Not wanting to look foolish, she passes the buck. "Our young friend over here," thumbing toward me, "must be a little early."

She signals me, and I obediently follow back to the front gate. "Listen, Stretch, sit tight here until the trainer arrives. He'll take you back to the classrooms."

I wade in cautiously, "If it's all the same to you, I think I'll go grab a cup of coffee."

"Suit yourself," Sheila lets me out the bolted door, and I go to my car to thumb through a book I find under my seat and try to kill an hour.

My reentry at five to nine is greeted by a coy smile from Sheila as she buzzes me in without a word. Evidently, Larry is in on the joke as he faintly waves upturned palms smirking, "You know the drill."

I'm a couple feet into the hallway when I turn to Larry, "Where's Annex G?"

"You follow this hallway down until it opens into a big corridor. Turn right, and you'll see a big red G painted on the wall. As soon as you enter that wing, the classroom will be on your right."

"Thanks." I leave Larry with a military salute that I've trademarked to show respect to my comrades through the years.

Larry should moonlight as a cartographer because his directions are dead on. I am weary of wandering around a secure adult facility unaccompanied, but Larry did me a solid. Entering the classroom, I'm greeted with a blast of AC that helps me understand the illustrative marketing of mint flavored gum. A rickety hum draws my eyes upward. I doubt warmth is coming any time soon, so I'll need to remember a jacket tomorrow.

"I asked them to turn it off while we're in here. Come up and sign in." An older, portly fellow motions me to the front of the class with the wave of a pen.

I've always been self-conscious, being a big guy, navigating through the tight rows of desks in a classroom. I'm not very nimble and can't shake the fat kid self-image of my youth. My fears are justified as I catch the corner of a desk but recover with a double hop on my right foot. As I turn to find a seat halfway back, I'm greeted by half-a-dozen melancholic faces who do not share my enthusiasm for what is about to transpire.

The class begins with a short overview from the instructor. Mr. Kennard explains he is up from the capitol, and he will be here for exactly half of our <u>five</u> day training (I have to call in to tell Mike this is not four days long). His partner, Mr. Danielson, will be relieving him halfway through Wednesday. Mr. Kennard assures us that, though he won't be here, we will be dismissed before lunch on Friday.

As he's delivering his spiel, a roll of toilet paper is circulated with the instructions, "Take what you would need for a two-day camping trip." Some are quite liberal; good for them for being so regular. I take four sheets knowing the amount is going to have to do with some kind of icebreaker.

As he finishes, Mr. Kennard accepts the roll back and breaks off three pieces explaining, "For each piece, you must share a fact about yourself. I am six months away from retirement. I have worked for the state 32 years. I married my high school sweetheart. Let's go around the room, and for those who have quite the pile, I'd use two to tell us your first and last name." Everyone gets a chuckle and the first hour passes swiftly.

Forty-five minutes into the activity, our last straggler arrives just before ten. I find out through his windedly embarrassed introduction that he is a teacher from my sister facility Janesville. Mr. Kennard reassures everyone that he will not be reporting to our supervisors but to be respectfully on time nonetheless.

It amuses me as we crack the binding of our one-inch-thick manual we received as a door prize that the first section is labeled

"Professionalism." Half the class poured in between five and fifteen minutes late.

Our conversation starts with dating in the workplace and escalates to sexual harassment. In an overly PC world, Mr. Kennard simplifies the definition. "It is not your intention. It's the other person's perception. Repeated and unwanted is the key."

"How do we know if it's unwanted?" A suave young man asks. His confidence is undermined by the fact that he may actually need to know this.

"I know it's hard to find Mr. or Mrs. Right nowadays," continues Kennard, "so read the signals, and especially if she says something, know when to back off. This can be a touchy subject. If you are offended, do your best to explain your feelings to the perpetrator the first time. That way you'll have a precedent and have given the person a chance before you involve a supervisor. The key is document, document, document. Whether completing a disciplinary ticket or any other incident report, if it's not written down, it never happened."

Training Week: Wednesday

A guy could get used to this schedule. I wake up later, get home earlier, and the drive time is just a shade longer. Having to work only six hours a day, one of which is lunch, has its perks. Having established a level of comfort with our trainer, I observe that the schedule is the model of inefficiency. Mr. Kennard enlightens me, "Well, young man, that's just how our fine state works. See, we could never ask you to do anything that would be outside the parameters of your agreed upon contract. So, for these training days, if we start an hour late and dismiss you an hour early, that usually covers the extra drive time for people and most won't request a state transport. Otherwise, we have to debate and argue over every extra minute and file for overtime. This is actually a rare instance of the state doing the right thing. Plus, it leaves you newbies feeling all warm, tingly, and loyal."

During one of our four breaks, I inquire as to how I could work my way into becoming a trainer. I contend having a background in education would make me a great fit. "They are a hot ticket, as you can tell," Kennard explains. "I've never seen a trainer in this position with less than 25 years of seniority. It is a lot of peoples' dream to sail out this way."

His advice, while jollily delivered, crosses that possibility off my list. One of the perks of switching to state retirement is I will be able to collect a pension before then. I want to become an old dusty professor, but it won't be in this capacity.

The training today revolves around offender interaction, de-escalation, and emergency response. In general, the teaching / interaction portions last 45 minutes or less and are broken up and supplemented by videotapes that are no less than 30 years old. Two of the tapes are repeats from my Annual Compliance Training.

These video portions include watching several uncomfortably cheesy reenactments of possible incidences we may encounter. The class's job is to gather enough information to write a concise incident report. I've already completed over a dozen of these, after which my boss, the chief of security, or other supervisory personnel

116

handed them back to me and explained a variety of conflicting ways I needed to amend each. Kennard thinks I'm the star student, finishing very quickly and being descriptive, yet succinct. He encourages me to circulate and help people who have questions. Kindly, he wants me to realize my training dream if only for a moment.

Intermission occurs when Kennard hands Mr. Danielson the baton. They greet like brothers united, exchange pleasantries, and then discuss what is left to cover for the third day of training:
Danielson: "So you introduced them to all the DO's?"
Kennard: "Yup."
Danielson: "Did you watch the 'Socialization' video?"
Kennard: "Affirmative."
Danielson: "Did you get to reporting?"
Kennard: "Yes indeed. In fact, they have each written three reports."
Danielson: "Which scenarios did you go through?"
Kennard: "The school fight, the dietary robbery, and the dayroom hustle."
Danielson: "All classics. Good choices. What haven't you covered?"
Kennard: "You could show them the prison takeover."
Danielson: "They won't report back to their posts!"
Kennard: "I know," holding in a belly laugh.
Danielson: "So, what am I supposed to teach them this afternoon?"
Kennard: "I don't know. Share from your wealth of knowledge and experience. You'll figure something out."
"Well kiddos," Danielson acknowledges our eves-dropping, "take 90 for lunch, and I'll see if I can muster up something for this afternoon."

The carnival of trainees finishes the parade back to our seats an hour and forty-five minutes later. Mr. Danielson doesn't notice the tardiness and delays another five minutes before announcing, "Is everybody present and accounted for?" Several people review the room, using our newly acquired detective skills to search for signs of

117

a missing body. "Good," our trainer neither waits for nor cares for a response.

Mr. Danielson regales us with his years of experience in a plethora of positions and facilities. Danielson entertains himself and some of us with his top-ten list of security gone haywire stories. The most memorable includes two staff members taken hostage. "It is in your best interest to cooperate as much as possible with the person holding the weapon." The possibility of being taken hostage pushes the conglomerate to evaluate our mortality as he continues, "It's our job to minimize the impact, so if you get a chance, break off your keys in a door to prevent further passage. There is a special notch in the door keys to make this easy." He pulls out a set as he navigates the room, "If you're outside, it is advantageous to chuck your keys on the roof."

Someone inquires, "Won't that just piss them off?"

"Studies have shown that once a plan is no longer feasible, perpetrators surrender before incurring more trouble. They may be mad but will rarely take it out on you because they figure they'll likely be caught and don't want to add a body or a beating to the attempted escape charge." Danielson delivers this terrifyingly risky maneuver with sociopathically sterile precision.

A middle-aged, buxom lady furthers the line of questioning; "Is there a time you should attempt to fight back?"

"For the most part, no." Danielson stares off while rubbing his chin. "Most inmates have a goal in mind and won't give you a second glance if you don't get in their way. If you present an obstacle, now they have to get through you."

"Wouldn't the keys be an obstacle?" The first questioner seems bent on invalidating the merits of such heroics.

"Not in that case. A perpetrator can get past an obstacle. What you have created is an impenetrable wall, and said inmate will have to rethink and perhaps give up the plans. You may get a smack, but the hopelessness of the situation will drain the offender of testosterone and aggression and leave them impotent."

"What if their goal is rape?" The bosomy lady's mousy tone crackles trying to deliver the question.

"The studies have conflicted in that area." Danielson stares off searching for a sensitive delivery. "At first, they said to fight back, but women were getting battered and still having to submit. Now, the official recommendation is to submit, but I can't see how anyone could live with that trauma. I guess you have to come to peace with what you would do in that situation and pray to God it never happens."

Danielson lets the somber moment hang as nobody can come up with a more pertinent question. "Well that's all I have. Stick around for 20 minutes and you can be dismissed at two." The once jovial group spends the remainder of the day pondering the possible traumas that await our current career track.

Evidently, two o'clock is the time security changes the guard. The doe-eyed trainees are forced to elbow their way through a feeding frenzy of key and radio returns to get out the door. I'm almost driven off the road from both sides as the exodus peels out of the parking lot.

High-Five-Half-Day Friday!!!

I choose to play the fool to celebrate the near completion of our training. Running up and down the aisles, I offer each classmate a raised palm. Unanimous participation and several smiles are my reward, and Danielson even participates with an enthusiastic slap.

The jubilation is stalled by our unsettling topics of conversation: rape, suicide, and anger management. We clearly find that sodomy is not the way as Danielson educates us on the federal laws that have been implemented to reduce and eliminate sexual assaults for wards of the state. *How bad had things gotten for this to be addressed at the federal level?*

Much of the discussion revolves around the signs of the already abused. Being a victim of rape is the number one cause of suicides in prison. The helplessness of having all freedoms removed skyrockets when such a violent invasion of intimate space occurs. There is no hiding it. Victims are almost always dramatically changed, and that is reflected in the inmates habits. Has a quiet person gotten loud or vice versa? Is there dramatic weight loss or gain? Are feelings of intense depression and hopelessness or a general lethargy present? Some can become very angry and aggressive to overcompensate for their inability to defend the attack and as a preventative measure against future incidents. This is all way too heavy for a squirrely group watching the hands of the clock inch closer to the weekend.

Danielson senses he's lost the crowd and releases us at 11:30 instead of working through lunch. Only foregoing one topic, most feel that training has been fulfilled, but I know from experience the importance of 'Health & Wellness.'

As a developing teacher, I found it incredibly difficult to shake off the day's work. Many days, I'd head straight to the couch, drink through dinner, and pass out with little recollection of the final hours of the night. To start the next day, I needed a heap of grease and a hot cup of fast food to make it back into work. The increasing frequency of my hangovers didn't improve the conditions of my classroom, and my ballooning body didn't diminish my depression. Our facility was paid to house the worst possible population outside

120

of prison, so education wasn't a top priority. As I lost motivation, the amount of time my students spent in front of movies or, yes, playing video games increased.

I can't quite say how I managed to find the other side. Thirty-five pounds lighter and having made peace with my creator, there was never a particular moment of epiphany, clarity, or comfort. I guess hopelessness became normal, and I learned to live with it.

<u>**Day 57**</u>

Got a case of the Mondays.

Last week's staycation training, compounded by the two-and-a-half day weekend that my wife and I spent at a friend's lake house, leaves me ill-equipped to dig back into the trenches. A sense of foreboding accompanies me on my walk to the school, and I resolve to give the kids a softball lesson to ease our way back in. I'm hoping they appreciate the gift and give me a break.

First block runs smooooth as every young man completes his work quietly and engages in muted, yet surprisingly appropriate, conversations for the remaining half hour. The impending parole board has the hopefuls on their best Sunday morning behavior.

During second block, I run headlong into a big "FUCK YOU!" Darnell Higgins decides to tag his desk instead of writing down the answers the class is completing as a group, OUT LOUD! I stare straight at him while he's sketching. He meets my gaze and continues.

I'm not even upset about the blatant disrespect. He'll get flagrant with the wrong person and receive a life lesson he won't soon forget (Karma can be comforting). I'm pissed about the extra paperwork I have to detail because this kid's a tool. This compounds with the truckload of special ed. caseloads dumped on me this morning because the JACKASS of a retired teacher, Ms. White, left after two months of failing to complete her responsibility. Mind you, Mike wants them completed yesterday, and I've never even seen, much less been trained on, how to construct them.

Presently, I use my non-existent artistic talents to copy down worthless gang graffiti in the attempt to stick it to this kid hard enough to encourage him to stop FUCKING with me.

The thought of silky, buttery popcorn dramatically improves my outlook. I head to our vending machines for lunch hoping I have enough on my money card (can't carry cash in prison) for a microwave bag.

Not one but TWO packages of popcorn get stuck in the machine. I was hopeful the second would push the first out. I debate my options and their possible outcomes. I can hungrily walk to the admin building and fill out a request for reimbursement, and they can add the two plus dollars onto my next paycheck. I can go for 'three's the charm,' but that might invalidate my claim to admin. I attempt to reach over the top corners and rock the machine. The amount of force needed gives me the distinct fear of being crushed. I settle for the kick-and-pray method, pausing for passersby. After eight attempts, I give up, paranoid that one of three witnesses may comment about my pounding.

My efforts are to no avail. It's an accumulation of days like today that lead some educators to turn on autopilot and coast for years to retirement.

My day slightly brightens when Mr. Frank shares I don't have to catch up on much grading. I left him with a packet-a-day for each of my 23 students to complete in the library in my absence. What did I get back? One packet. One out of 92.

I envision some downtrodden Native American in the middle of wilderness shedding a tear. Fret not, my friend! The material was on your people's history, once again, disregarded.

Day 58

Special education has become an intentionally generic field. In the past, teachers had to get endorsed in the specific disability category they were planning to instruct. Because of the rapid growth of special education services, all disability categories fall under the academic umbrella of "Learning Behavior Specialist" (LBS1). With these qualifications, an educator can school any persons between the ages of 3 and 21 with disabilities ranging from complete paralysis to Down's syndrome, behavior disorders to high-functioning autism, and everything in between.

Predictably, each special educator gravitates toward a population with which they are comfortable and experience success. Inevitably, each teacher has certain students that make him or her feel inadequate. My student is Karl Bagwell.

Karl stomps the halls with an impressive fro that waves to the rhythm of his pounding. Karl routinely clenches his fists and has a permanent scowl on his face. At first sighting, I thought he was hunting to beat the living daylights out of someone. Considering this impression, I aim to not be that person.

Karl was recently added to my roster. He came in and took a desk right in front of me, consistently scowling and glowering. Not at me, through me.

Karl doesn't acknowledge the existence of life around him. Any question directed at him receives a twenty to thirty second delay followed by a grunt or one word answer that often needs to be deciphered before a connection to the material can be endeavored. I have to remind Karl to copy down notes on the board each and every time something is added. After a thirty second delay, he looks down, grabs his pencil, squints at the notes, writes on the page, squints at the notes, and writes on the page.

At the culmination of the period, each student returns his folder to a bin on my desk, and of course, Karl needs prompting and a grace period to comply. When I check his assignment, very few words are discernable. From what I can gather, Karl's writings are in no way connected to any assignment we've completed. Do I fail him for not being able to copy my written notes, or is this the best he can do? Going with a "C" minus, I resolve that he'll have to put together a cogent sentence to argue for a higher mark.

Day 61

Fourth block is infused with energy when Antwon Bates curtly launches his textbook, folder and pencil off the wall, "You wanna fuckin fight! I'll find yo ass on the street! You and your wife! We'll run a train on that ho!" *Hot Button*

During a training on antecedent triggers, the lecturer instructed everyone to stand and gravitate toward whichever sidewall fit their level of discomfort. The wall stage right was a one signifying very comfortable, and the wall to the left was a ten, meaning that it is in our best interest to excuse ourselves before we lose control. We started out easy with insolence and cursing. Moving into threats and intimidation, people started getting edgy. Physical assault was the pinnacle of this line of inquiry, and I was interrogated by the presenter about why this bothered me so little. "I get a headache from all the lip-smacking. I've done physical management for a while and am confident in my ability to deescalate a situation." The presenter jutted out her lip, impressed, and moved onto sexual harassment.

I found, to my surprise, biting and spitting to be revulsive to me, even more than smearing feces (that really happens). But, the most unnerving was threats to loved ones. I make my peace and build my strength on the separation of home and work. When those walls come down, a lion-like defensive aggression saturates my body.

Trying my hardest not to flinch or flush and reveal this youth got to me, I calmly and politely ask him to leave. "Please, step outside, Mr. Bates."

"Fuck you, bitch! Make me!" Another source of enticement. I am a rather large individual, and when an insolent young man who is 50 pounds my junior asks me to "make him," I'm quite tempted to oblige.

"Mr. Bates, step out." I increase the terseness of the message while trying to remain composed.

"Fuck yo bitch ass!" Bates leans back and crosses his arms, "You can't make me do shit!"

126

Waving a guard over, I explain that a student has earned a referral and refuses to leave. I point out Bates and direct my attention to my desk to not escalate the situation further. "See, yo pussy ass has to call in yo boyfriend. Try and flex on me. See whatchoo get!" Bates makes a faint like he's going to rush my desk but exits with a cocky smirk. I try to recall as much of his phraseology as possible to quote on the disciplinary ticket.

This episode began because Mr. Bates requested to use the locked washroom. During the previous two days, Bates sat sideways in his chair, gang-banging and threatening all present with a variety of violent acts using a myriad of weapons until he was asked to leave. Today, I explained I would open the washroom when and if Mr. Bates could gather his materials and remain on-task for ten straight minutes. This tactic has worked well in the past because once a student is invested in the work, his self-worth increases, and he usually wants to continue the successful behavior. I reiterate: usually.

Mr. Bates requested to use the washroom six times, oblivious to the repetition of my response. When I stopped engaging him, he did sit down but quickly asked, "Why the fuck isn't the bathroom open?" I calmly restated the expectation, and after enough of a delay to save face, Bates complied. He made it eight minutes before the unprovoked outburst.

Regaling Casey Sawyer with my story, he has little empathy. "Go talk to Mike to seal the deal. Get him out of your class. That kid's fucked in the head. When I tried the same maneuver of ignoring him, he waited a good long while until I forgot and then sent a literature textbook Frisbeeing over my head."

"And he's still here after trying to assault you?" Typically a staff assault or attempt is a surefire ticket to a different facility.

"Where's he gonna go?" Casey illuminates an unsettling truth, "We talked to his counselor about a transfer, but he just gets bounced back. The max facility says he's too 'special treatment,' and the special treatment facility says he's too 'violent.' So, he gets to stay with us. The worst part is Bates pulls a stunt like this every four to six weeks, and our inability to consequence him just escalates it. Did you hear he chased a female guard down the hallway of Madison with his dong out, stroking it?"

127

"Disgusting!" My revulsion triggers my stomach to turn when this news is combined with his threats to my wife.

"If that didn't get him booted, your issues are small peanuts, man. The best thing you can do is get him removed from your class." Casey's 'pass the buck' advice, while practical, does not sit well with me, knowing I'm just unloading on some other poor soul.

My game plan approaching Mike is to show a pattern of attempted interventions and offer an escalative measure. Mike listens intently to my spiel and ponders my request to sit down with Bates and his counselor outside the classroom to process through the hindrances. "I've done it a lot in other placements with success," I appeal, "It wouldn't take long; I can have security watch my class."

"I'll set it up with Mr. Smithe." Mike smiles, and I hope that means he appreciates my efforts to think around the problem. He might just be giving me enough rope to hang myself by, but I have to try.

Mrs. Peters gives me directions through the labyrinth of the Clinic to find Mr. Smithe's office. I want to be on the same page and introducing myself to the person on which my boss just dumped my problems seems like a good first step.

"Yeah, Bates flagged me down today when I was making my rounds in Madison." Donald Smithe is a middle-aged, black man with a collection of professional sports teams' hats he uses to cover his shaved head. He lounges in his office with his feet on the desk and his hands over his midsection. "He gave me the same sob story about you being 'a bitchass nigga,' but I wasn't in the mood to deal with his bullshit. So, I told him to get off his usual crap and moved on to the next whiner."

Not sure how to ingratiate myself enough to make this request, I proceed timidly. "I was hoping for you to just be a quiet mediator as I talk through and get to the bottom of this issue with Bates."

"His issue is he's a whiney bitch whose mamma told him he was special." Mr. Smithe wastes no time sharing his philosophies on dealing with troubled youth.

"All the same," I attempt to regain the point, "I was hoping we could have a sit down. It seems like Mr. Bates isn't going anywhere any time soon, and I'm just trying to manage the situation the best I can."

"Yeah, Mr. Hicks told me your idea. I doubt it'll work, but I'm game. Have him set it up." Returning his feet to the floor, Smithe leans forward to extend a hand, and we part ways shaking amicably.

Day 63

Monday comes and goes without a Bates sighting or further communication from Mike. I figure if Bates isn't in my class, my problems are solved. I made an effort, and I'm getting the impression that's all that matters around here.

This afternoon as I pass through the foyer on the way upstairs, Mr. Smithe happens to be passing through and makes me a proposal. "Bates is stuck in Truman because he blacked a kid's eye. I've got a couple minutes before I have to lead conferences on Madison. If you're up for a walk, I'll give you a tour of the labyrinth that is our confinement, and we can chat up your boy." Having no other pressing matters, I thank him and oblige he lead the way.

Boy's Home isolation cells are connected to the infirmary for good reason. Most of the inhabitants are there for fighting. Between the altercation itself and the subsequent manhandling from the guards, it saves time to have medical personnel close for evaluations.

A Youth Correction Officer buzzes us in through two sets of doors. Mr. Smithe exchanges pleasantries and makes our request. The guard heads down a corridor filled with cells that differ from the houses. The smell of urine permeates the whole place; evidently pissing on the walls is a form of social protest for the wrongfully imprisoned. Each cell is very Spartan with a single, metal bunk affixed to the wall and no stool, table or shelves to adorn it. The door has a small latch that opens into the hallway, I presume to pass food trays in and out. I see a set of hands stick out the latch, and the guard shackles the wrists before opening the door. Bates glowers as he heads towards us with his hands pinned behind his back.

Mr. Smithe leads us into a room that can't be more than six by six where an unneeded desk makes things more claustrophobic. I take the seat behind the desk ensuring a barrier between myself and Bates. Despite being shackled, Bates exudes an intention to do me harm given any opportunity.

"What the fuck do you want?" Bates snarls as he sits on a bench affixed to the wall.

130

"Pump your breaks, Bates. Mr. Masters is just here to talk." Mr. Smithe postures on the corner of the desk with arms crossed to stare down at our youth.

"I don't give a fuck! His bitchass is the reason I'm in here." Bates seethes the accusation at me.

"Don't bullshit him," Smithe calls Bates to the carpet. "You clocked a kid; that's why you're here."

"After this pussy kicked me out of class," Bates is perched on the very edge of the bench and looks ready to leap at Smithe.

"That's why I'm here, Mr. Bates," I attempt to derail this train wreck. "I want to figure out how to help you be successful in my class."

"Fuck your class! I don't need school. I'm a whole ass nigga!" I get the impression that if his hands were available, he'd pound his chest for emphasis.

"I can understand that school isn't your thing. But, you're assigned to my class, and I think it would keep you in less trouble if you were able to stay in class the whole period. What can we do to make that happen?" I extend an opportunity for him to share his needs in hopes that an adult with a listening ear can break through.

"Your class doesn't matter." He settles back against the wall, frustrated. "My therapist and Smithe's bitchass won't listen to me."

"Watch it." Smithe growls, still trying to assert his dominance.

"Please be respectful Mr. Bates. Continue," I prod.

"I lost my phone call cuz some false flaggin motherfucker put me on blast." He opens up despite my failure to comprehend of the gravity of losing a phone call.

"I can understand why losing a privilege is upsetting to you. Is there any way you can separate that anger from what's happening in class? Is that peer in my class with you?" I attempt to get Bates to compartmentalize his rage to establish a separate, safe space in my room.

"No." Bates droops into a posture that might indicate he's about to cry. The adrenaline from all that anger drains into a helpless realization as he sits there on his hands.

"Good. I hope you can work it out with that peer and earn another phone call." Wrapping up, "Next time you come to class, can you grab your materials and find a seat quietly?" No response. "Even if you don't want to participate, having your materials makes you look like you're making an effort. If you can sit in your assigned classroom quietly, I don't see why you'd lose any points." Bates stares blankly at the base of the desk not registering that I'm talking, "If you need a break, you can ask to talk to your youth correctional officer."

"CO don't wanna hear shit!" I've touched a sore spot. "'Go to class; do your work,'" Bates mimics commands he's heard. "They don't fuckin listen." His expression is more exasperation than anger. He perceives that there's no legitimate outlet and therefore lashes out like a cornered animal.

"I'm sorry to hear you're having issues with your staff." Bates looks me in the eye, just for a moment, and I can tell I'm making a dent. "How about just laying your head on the desk until you feel ready? Taking a five to ten minute quiet break is okay."

Bates is back to staring at the floor. I perceive his lack of response as a lack of objection, so I take my chips and run. "I'll see you tomorrow, hopefully. Remember, if you don't bother the class, I won't bother you. Just tell me if you need something." I look to Smithe to wrap things up. He pounds on the glass of the door leading out of this shoebox. Evidently, we've been locked in here the whole time. We let Bates lead the way, and the guard secures him and removes the handcuffs before letting us out.

I thank Mr. Smithe before we head in opposite directions. He leaves me with endearing assurance, "I doubt he heard half of what you said. That kid's in his own universe. Let me know if he gives you any more problems." Smithe backs away, giving me the peace sign before turning on his heel and fading into the horizon.

Entering the school building, I bump into Mike and report on my progress to relay that he no longer needs to call a meeting and collect some easy brownie points. "Oh, good," Mike hazily recollects the details of our previous conversation, "So, Bates is on board?"

"We'll have to wait and see." I leave myself an out because there is no telling what this kid will do. I've laid the groundwork and, from the look of it, made more of an attempt than anyone else ever has. If it doesn't work out, I've made a great case for Mr. Bates to get bounced from my class. "I set some clear, achievable expectations. It is up to Mr. Bates to comply." Mikes seems content with this answer and returns to leafing through his mail on the way to his office.

Day 64

Today, being the final day of the month, Mike is contractually required to run the monthly a staff meeting before the clock strikes four. There is nothing on the official calendar, and Mr. Park and Mrs. Wells, our union representation, are wringing their hands in the hopes of trapping Mike. They're sorely disappointed when youth are dismissed at the end of the first block.

Mike convenes us in the education office to pass out an agenda still warm from the copier. "First, I believe congratulations are in order." Mike extends an open palm to Santarini who takes a slight dramatic bow from his chair. "After thirty-two?" Mike looks inquisitively towards Santa.

"Thirty-three," Santa corrects.

"After thirty-three years of service with city public schools and another eight teaching here, Mr. Santarini will be retiring from teaching today." It is uncomfortable to watch these two feign comradery when everyone knows the not-so-veiled contempt they've publicly shared about one another. "What's next, Burt?"

"My wife and I have a two week cruise booked the day after tomorrow," Santa boasts while raising his posture. "When I get back, I'll have to straighten some things out, but don't worry; I intend to come back as a tutor for a couple hours a week."

"That would be nice," Mike contemptuously smiles. "The retirement party will be in the conference room at the front gate. Remember not to leave your posts until 11:30, unless you're helping set up, and I expect everyone to be back by 12:30 sharp because we will be having school this afternoon." Mike gives a stern finger wag spanning the room. Any hope of a leisurely conclusion to the day is released with a chorus of groans.

Arriving to the gate at 11:40 to minimize my time in a large group setting, I'm unclear why four teachers had to leave at 11:00 because nothing is set up. Ms. Vasquez waves a food-soaked spoon to enlist my services, "Mr. Masters, could you be a doll and spread the tablecloths on each table?" There goes my plan to eat and run.

134

The masses pool in at noon, and the main courses of fried chicken and mostaccioli are delivered at ten past. I start to sweat the fact that I might have to eat on the walk back to school when Casey gives my shoulders a confident squeeze. "Relax, man. Mike gets off by being a prick. As long as he's down here, there is nothing to worry about." Casey nods to him behind us in line, "and Mike's never missed a free meal. Lunch is a religious experience for his tubby ass."

Casey and I make our way to a half-filled table of teachers. Ms. Brown and Mike join us, much to the chagrin of the others. Mike is cheery but makes no mention of delaying our start time as he tucks a napkin into his shirt collar.

The proceedings are started with a blessing from one of the union people who previously met me at the front gate passing out leaflets and insisting I call my state representative. Evidently he is the master of ceremonies and kicks things off by asking supervisors if they have any parting words. Three bosses make speeches, including the chief of security's banal recitation for Mr. Gagnon, my Compliance trainer. Mike reluctantly waddles his way to the mic to wrap up management's contribution.

"What can I say about Mr. Santarini?" His pause is too long and reveals that he may find it difficult to compliment his staff. "Santa, as the kids call him, came to us from the county lockup's school, the Otis House. Many a familiar face greeted him warmly upon his arrival here, and I think Burt enjoyed prolonging his relationships with the boys." The increasing awkwardness makes the whole room shift in their seats, but no one can look away. "Burt has been a valued asset on our team, and we'll miss you." Mike completes his summation with the bent-over hug of a seated Santarini that nearly sends them both toppling to the floor.

Mr. Andrews, our MC, retakes the mic to share a detailed, heart-felt story of his experience with each of the retirees before handing the mic over to them. Gagnon reluctantly starts by thanking his wife, daughter, and two grandchildren who are present before addressing the crowd. "It has been an honor to serve with you, my brothers and sisters, for 27 great years. We've had our moments, but I wouldn't trade them for anything in the world. I will leave you with this: you will not receive a lot of accolades from this job, which is a shame, but the restful sleep you get knowing you made a difference, changed a life, will bless you now and through eternity. Thank you for all the years, the laughs, and the tears." He gracefully waves goodbye as he settles back into his seat, wiping his cheek as a single tear escapes his eye.

Santa ho, ho, hums through a comedy routine that only he and the crickets find amusing before Mr. Andrews opens the mic up for coworkers to say a few words. Quickly making his way to the mic is an inner-city-reverend looking fella. He wears an all-black suit with a gold neck chain around his black turtleneck. A gold wrist watch and three gold rings glimmer his extremities and a gold tooth leaves me dubious to his message. "Congratulations retirees, new and old. Let's give them a hand." He holds the mic over his head to lead a golf-clap. "For those who don't know," he sneers thinking himself a celebrity, "I'm Jameson Francis, your local union representative and liaison to the fat-cats in the capitol." Bobbing his head and chortling, he appreciates his own dig. "While we have you gathered here, I wanted to give you an update the happenings upstate . . ."

"Hey, why don't you sit down!" A thirty something, athletically framed woman interrupts the preacher at his pulpit. "This lunch is supposed to be about them!"

"You are right, young lady," the minister gracefully affirms. "This is about them. We are in the fight of our lives down in the capitol. And it affects them, and you, and all of us. If we don't stand up and fight for what we've accomplished, what we deserve, it will be lost." Francis pauses to wipe his brow and receive affirmation. "I'm here to represent and protect these retirees' right to their pension and to ensure that there is still a pension when it's your turn, my young friend." He nods condescendingly to the interrupter to establish his experience and wisdom while putting the objector in her place. The provocation leads her to the purse her lips and cross her arms as an affirmation of defiance.

It's getting to be too much for me, so I elbow Casey and Ms. Vargas, and we slink out the back of the room to head back to the school.

It's half-past one when Mikes announces, *The houses will be up shortly.* I assume that the kids will head to their second class of the afternoon because by the time transition is done, it'll be that time.

This, of course, has not been communicated, and through a series of misfires, security yells the plan around the hallway to go to the first class.

Forty-five minutes after the first public service announcement and fifteen minutes past the usual class change time, our fearless leader elaborates, "*Youth should be in their 4th period class. The time now is for class change. Please proceed to your 5th period class.*" I notice Santa's door remains closed during the change. Using hand signals to question Mrs. Peters, she yells back, "He gets walked out after the party. Admin collects his keys and ID. There's no reason for him to come back. They think it hurts productivity."

And, a fine farewell to you, sir.

Day 67

"Well hello there, neighbor. Welcome back." I poke my head into 207 to find Mrs. McDonough has returned from Janesville.

She unenthusiastically twirls her finger, "Whoopee."

"Did you enjoy your time at our sister facility?" I endeavor to start a dialogue.

"It's better than this shit pit." At first take, I think she doesn't care for me.

"If you don't like it here, why didn't you stay over there?" I inquire innocently.

"Because the dumbass at Janesville who got hit in the head with a stapler is on paid leave. He's claiming mental duress on top of a dented skull, so they have to pay him for a year to sit on his ass. The position is reserved in case he feels like returning." I'm starting to think McDonough just has a downtrodden disposition, which makes her the perfect Yang to Mrs. Peters spunky Ying.

"Couldn't you sub there 'til he gets back?" I offer.

"I wish. But one, our useless union fights for what is written in the contract, in spite of what the union member wants. So, they won't let me. And two, Mike is paranoid about losing teachers, so he would never allow a long term stay anywhere else. Did you know he blocked Ms. Brown from getting a principal position at another facility?" She perks slightly to spread maliciousness.

Trying to turn the corner and retreat to my room, "Well, I'm glad you're back."

"Hey, what did you do with my kids while I was gone?" I forgot that Mike originally assigned me her class load.

"I talked to Mike about taking over Ms. White's kids when she left, so your boys have gone untouched. I'll get you your materials back at lunch." I'm pleased with myself that I skirted any uncomfortable comparisons by our shared youth.

"So, you're teaching history?" McDonough inquires.

"Yup," I'm chipper over my maneuvering.

"That's bullshit!" I've struck a nerve. "Mike knows he has to offer available subjects based on seniority. What if I wanted it?"

Her accusatory interrogation has me backpedaling. "We can switch if you want." *Please say no.*

"Forget it. Just another example of how I get screwed every time I walk in this place." McDonough dismisses me by opening a file folder. I catch a glimpse of Sudoku puzzles inside as I quietly exit.

"Jessi girl!!!" Mrs. Peters ecstatically reunites with her long lost counterpart.

"Hello Diane, dear. How I have missed you so." Mrs. McDonough answers coyly.

"Oh, there is just so much you've missed! Where to start?" I get the feeling I'm eavesdropping on a slumber party and wonder if closing my door would be perceived as rude. "Dirty old Santa finally retired."

"Good riddance," McDonough guffaws, "that guy would always tell me degrading stories about his wife and then hit on me. What a creep. Can you believe Mike's stupid ass gave me his kids?"

"No." Peters prods her girl onward.

"Yeah. Evidently, he didn't touch any of my kids, so they spent those weeks wasting away in the library. I'm sure they're gonna love that I'm back. And on top of that, Santarini's list is waiting in my mailbox. I'm gonna have the most students out of any special ed. teacher. Welcome fuckin back!"

I take this as my cue to put my lunch in the refrigerator, creating an opportunity to shut the door upon return.

Day 68

Taking over reading our textbook after thanking a volunteer, my periphery detects an airborne object. I jolt back in my chair, looking up to deflect what I think is being thrown at me, and I capture the tail end of the lofted candy bar landing on a student's desk. "Mr. Jackson, can you bring that to me?"

"See ,you done gone and fucked it up," Jackson scowls at the thrower.

"Why is candy flying across my classroom in the middle of reading?" I quiz.

"Jefferson wanted to trade me the chocolate for a G-shot I got." Jackson freely sells out his friend.

"G-shot?"

"Yeah, you know, of a girl's pussy." These young men are entirely too candid.

Blushing, "You guys aren't supposed to have that. Do I need to have you two searched?"

"Naw, naw. Here," Jackson produces several torn magazine pages from the front of his pants and attempts to shove them into my hand.

"I'm not touching that," and I'm afraid to look, but the young ladies appear to be covered in the right places, barely. "If it's allowed, why are you guys trading in my class?"

"Jefferson needs some fresh pics to beat his meat. I gotta hook up my boy." Jackson beams unabashedly.

"Shut the fuck up!" Jefferson pipes in, embarrassed. He makes no moves to recover his end of the deal.

"This conversation is not even close to appropriate to be having with a teacher, and I definitely don't want to hear about what you do all day in your room. So, here's the deal. If you both work the rest of the time without any problems," I eye Jefferson, "I will give you your candy bar as you are leaving. Next time you bring any outside stuff in, it will be treated as contraband, and I will confiscate it to attach to the disciplinary ticket. Do we understand each other?" Both nod emphatically and stare intently at their textbooks.

At the end of class, I call Jefferson to my desk and wait for a delaying Jackson to leave. "Have a nice day, Mr. Masters." He grins, ducking out.

"Jefferson, what are you doing?" I reproach a young man who has exhibited some potential. "There isn't some other way to get what you want than throwing candy bars across my class?"

"Sorry, Mr. Masters." He watches his feet shuffle sheepishly.

"I know we're in a tough environment here, but to be successful, you have to practice habits that you need for a better place than this. That doesn't include trading candy for pervy 'G-shots.'" I snicker to lighten the reproach. "Keep it in your pants, man."

Jefferson smirks at my adaptation of their lingo. "Sorry, Mr. Masters. It won't happen again."

"I'll let you go so you can catch Jacks to get your merch."

Jefferson slinks out the door, flashing one last cat-that-ate-the-canary grin before jetting down the hallway.

Day 70

Please see me about your balls. A note taped to the side of the mailbox wishes me a good morning. "Mike, you wanted to talk?"

"Yeah, come on in and sit down, Jon." Mike seems chipper, so I might survive this meet.

"Door open or closed?"

"Closed," I may have spoken too soon. "Have you made any progress on those balls?"

I parked them in an empty classroom hoping Mike would be retired before someone came across them. "Not yet. I've been trying to get my arms around my class and my SPED caseload." Casey shared that it is in my best interest to stress I have more on my plate than I can handle. If there is a hint of white space, Mike will pile on until the whole thing topples.

"Did you coordinate with Mr. Park about cutting the desks?" He continues.

"I haven't had the chance yet because I wanted to blow up a couple more to see if it's absolutely necessary," I extend the lie.

"Stay on top of that," Mike condescends before cheerily reminiscing, "I can't believe the months have passed so fast. It's time for your three month evaluation." I have not bolstered my case by disappointing the boss right out of the gate. Mike hands me a file. "Look over the form. I've circled your marks. If you agree, do nothing. If you feel you should get a higher or lower mark, indicate it by circling what you think you deserve."

I quickly scan the whole packet. Mike has given me all "S" for satisfactory on the four-and-a-half page evaluation. I pretend to read the headings and take the appropriate amount of time for Mike to think I thoroughly analyzed it. Signing and handing it back, I shamelessly brown nose, "Thanks for the opportunity here. I really am starting to enjoy myself, and I fully intend on spending the rest of my career here."

"Good," Mike is pleased with the interaction. I could've argued for a couple of 'excellent' marks, but Mike is the type to balance 'excellent' with 'needs improvement.' I figure I'm level right here. Plus, it looks like Mike cut and pasted my info onto a previous teacher's evaluation without changing or adding any comments. If I make him think, I'm sure his new judgement will not err in my favor. Discretion is best utilized to fight another day.

Day 71

In an effort to further the Strategic Behavior Systems initiative or just to spot-check compliance, Mike uses today's teacher institute to request a copy of each teacher's classroom rules. Every staff meeting I've attended has included a reminder that clearly posted, consistently enforced expectations are the cornerstones of SBS. Mike's guidelines are vague at best, only instructing us to include the three P's (prepared for class, promoting respect, and proactively safe) with an explanation of what that looks like in our classrooms. Requiring us to turn these in is a little juvenile, but the stairs make a long trip for hefty Mike to check class by class. Additionally, that leaves him in a weak position visiting our domains. He insists upon individual conferences in his den to reassert his prowess.

"What is an 'Achievement of the Week'?" Mike scrutinizes my list.

"Even the worst kids can have a shining moment," I explain. "I try to pick one such instance from my morning and one from my afternoon classes. I transcribe the incident onto a certificate and give it to the student with a treat."

"That's what the Terrific Tokens are for, Jon," Mike condescends, stringently holding to the established reward system.

Reassuring him, "I use those, too. This is just another way to define and highlight those accomplishments. A step further, if you will. I give the student a certificate and display another copy for a couple of weeks as an example to motivate other students. It is my goal to display six to eight different students at a time, and I vary the reason for the success to motivate the kids to go beyond the basic expectations."

Mike is uncomfortable with the idea that I've expanded upon his status quo. I've always been suspicious that he doesn't quite understand the intricacies of behavior modification. Strategic Behavior Systems and programs like it are a platform to create a culture of encouragement. Mike is a leftover from the old regime when adult and juvenile prisons followed the same rules. The years of stringent protocols have engrained in him the necessity to follow the letter of the law, which is contradictory to SBS's intent.

"What's 'Hard Work Hump Day' and 'Hooray 'A' Friday?'" He continues feigning curiosity to mask his discomfort.

144

"Well, I've noticed Wednesdays are difficult to get through. The kids have had a couple days of school and have a couple more 'til the weekend. It's just a friendly prompt to buckle down even when the motivation's not there. Kids who complete their work and exhibit compliance are rewarded with a quarter size piece of candy." I wait to see if Mike will hassle me for sneaking in outside treats.

He reserves his judgment as I press on. "Similarly, I want the boys to value academic achievement. Every Friday, I update their grades to instill accountability. They can track the fluctuations, and I can conference with them to connect the ups and downs to the week's work. For those who have an A, giving them a small treat reinforces the importance of their grades and incentivizes peers to take school seriously."

"And you think that works?" Mike is doubtful that any of the boys find school important. To him, they're just playing a role to get paroled.

"I've seen it," I contend. "I've seen rough and tumble kids become studious on Wednesdays. Even if they're failing, they work that one day a week for a small treat. Some even pledge to get an Achievement Certificate. And, kids who didn't attend school for months on the outside are taken aback when they receive an A in class. For some, this is the first time they've found success in school."

Mike does not know what to do with me. This conference is meant for correction and the assertion of his authority, but I've broadened his scope, which makes him uneasy. He approves my form with one last gibe. "This will work. Just take out the 'pleases' for me."

"Excuse me?" I'm unclear what he's asking.

"Your explanation of our directives has 'pleases' here and here." He points to my respectful emphases of the important bullet points. "These kids are our prisoners, Jon. We shouldn't have to ask them 'please' because it displays weakness on our part."

Floored by such a blatantly diminished view of our wards, this affirms my belief that Mike doesn't grasp the programming he's pushing. I'm starting to appreciate the overwhelming dissension among the teaching staff. There is no reasoning with our principal.

"Okay," I withdrawal. "I've won the war, so forfeiting this last battle to reassure Mike seems strategically advantageous.

Day 73

A respectful looking youth knocking at the door and holding a plate covered with what looks to be mashed baked goods provides my first period class with a much needed break. "How can I help you, young man?"

"Mr. Sawyer wanted me to offer you a piece of his birthday cake." The boy extends the offering to me, which I cautiously yet graciously accept.

"Tell him I send my fondest birthday wishes and appreciate his generosity." I excuse the messenger with a seated dramatic bow.

"What the hell did you give me?" I immediately accost Sawyer after dismissal. I'm not sure if or when food poisoning will kick in, but if this is hazing, I want to know what I'm in for.

"So you ate it?" he laughs. "I wasn't sure you'd trust an inmate messenger."

"You're about to find out when I chuck it all over your class," I fake a convulsion.

"Relax, the boys never touched it." Casey keeps his casually cool demeanor despite my digestive alarms.

"What was in that?"

"Well," Casey muses, leaning forward to count the ingredients on his fingers, "the base of it is processed and packed cinnamon rolls. From there we added candy-coated chocolate, individual packets of peanut butter, honey and jelly, and a small box of rice cereal. We put it all in a Ziploc, very hygienic," giving me the OK sign reassuringly, "and poured a carton of milk and some water over the top before mashing it. We used a text book to flatten it before sliding it out onto a plate. And, voila! You have yourself a prison cake."

"Why? Just why?" I cannot fathom what would motivate the youth, much less a teacher, to do such a thing.

"These kids get bored with the mundane. They have to spice things up and creatively use the resources at their disposal," Casey shrugs.

146

"Why would you want to eat it? And share it?" I'm still slightly disgusted by what I've ingested.

"The kids found out it was my birthday and wanted to honor me. Do you know how difficult it is for these boys to think about anyone but themselves? They came together, each bringing ingredients, to hand make me a gift. It's touching when you think about it." Casey smiles as he pretends to wipe away a tear. "At least it's not the taco pushup fiasco."

"The what, now?" Just when I start to assimilate a new concept, Casey drops another on me unexpectedly.

"Yeah," he chuckles, "I had a kid who offered to do 500 pushups in 24 hours if his roommate would give him a taco."

"Taco?" I need a notepad.

"Yeah, short for walking tacos; the kids can order tortilla chips and packets of squeeze cheese off their commissary. They crunch the chips, pop the bag, and drizzle the cheese over the top." Casey animates the process for my benefit. "It's all the rage. Anyway, so this kid makes it to about 350 before lights out and figures he'll wake his roommate to count the nighttime sessions. About 1:30, a blood curdling shriek sends the guards racing to his room. The young man can't get out of bed. They send him first to our infirmary and then by ambulance to the local hospital all while he screams through every twitch."

"You're kidding?" This story is too sensational to be a fallacy.

"I wish for his sake I was. He comes back to us after three days of heavy sedation and hourly, full-body ice baths. He has to stay on the infirmary because between separating the pec's connection to his left arm and completely tearing his right tricep, he has to be slung and mummified at all times. Picture having to take a shower or shit. I would hate to be the guard who drew that duty."

"Unbelievable."

"And get this. Six weeks later when he gets back to Jefferson House, his roommate has been paroled. He never got the taco." Casey softly chuckles as he throws a chocolate in the air and catches it in his mouth.

The afternoon is devoid of IEP meetings so we can spend some face time with the SPED director for the state and receive training. The training comes as surprise to me heading to my classroom after

147

lunch. The accepted practice of instantaneous schedule changes still irks me.

I get anxious at these things because SPED paperwork and laws are constantly in flux. I feel like a fraud when I learn the new guidelines and picture having to redo all the files that are not up to date. So far, I've never been called on it, but it still makes me worry.

"For those who don't know," scanning the room and settling on me, "I think you're the only new face, I'm Sheila Sass," she throws her hips around to amply justify such a boisterous name, "the Special Services Director for the state."

"Before we start," Sheila continues, "did y'all get my gifts?"

"What gifts?" Mrs. McDonough pipes in.

"The computers and printers I purchased for each of you." Her hands float whimsically by her side as if she is a fairy about to grant a wish.

"Yeah, they came alright." McDonough loves dishing on the dirt. "They're useless because the state can't find the software that was purchased to load onto them."

"I bought them eight months ago," Sheila protests with less whimsy, more petulance.

"The investigation is ongoing." McDonough delivers the sarcastic punchline with biting comedic timing.

"Have you been able to use the two projectors I sent?" Sass cautiously continues.

McDonough carries on, enjoying the lively conversation in place of a tedious training. "Mike's got those locked away in his office. He says we can sign one out, but that's a royal hassle. The other one was borrowed by the administration building and returned broken."

"I'll see if we can free them up and get admin to replace the other." She's back to godmother with a sternly protective tone. "What about the blowup balls for the kids to sit on." So, she is the one who started all this.

I field her query. "I blew a couple up, but they're too small for the desks we have."

"Did you ask Mike to return them and exchange for a larger set?" She might not be aware of Mike's strict policies against common sense.

"Yeah, but Mike wants the woodshop teacher to saw down the legs of all the tables instead," I enlighten her.

"Ridiculous!" seamlessly transitioning to British nanny, "I'll get to the bottom of this, straight away!" She harrumphs to punctuate her point and segues into our training. Evidently, she went to a three-day seminar on laws and procedures when the state couldn't afford to send us all for training. Instead, she has been commissioned to boil the material down to a 90 minute presentation. Proceeding to this position from a very well put-together special ed. consortium, I find I've been well trained and use my knowledge to support Ms. Sass and assist my peers in framing our new responsibilities.

At the conclusion of the demonstration, Ms. Sass motions me over for an overdue introductory handshake. "You seem to know your way around the material. I'm impressed. You know; I will be retiring in the next two years, and they'll be searching for a new director."

"I'll definitely think about it," I kindly oblige her noncommittally. I don't have the relationship with her to explain that I'm not the administrative type at this point. I've seen way too many young teachers climb out the classroom too early only to get burnt out under the burden of management or hit a ceiling and be stuck in a position they hate. I'm happy where I'm at and figure I'll save changing the world for the last five to ten years of my career. That way if I make a decision that gets me ridden out of town, I'll be uninhibited enough to go out in a blaze of glory.

Night 74

WE'RE HAVING A BABY!!!

My intuition gives me the good news as I talk to Annie on my car ride home. She quizzes me as to when her monthly ritual was supposed to commence, and I tell her a week ago.

"Do you think I'm pregnant?" She asks vacillating between excitement and terror.

"Yep." I'm confident that my mathematical skills to prevent pregnancy over our first several years of marriage have been reversed to lead us to our current state.

"Should I take a test?" Annie quivers with uncertainty.

"That would be good," I laugh. She can't see, but I'm beaming. I've always wanted to have kids. We waited until our late twenties to get our finances in order and enjoy the married life a little. My stomach flutters in my chest.

"What should we do if we're pregnant?" Annie's mind has temporarily melted down from trying to process the possibility.

"How about I take you out to dinner?" I offer.

"Sounds good," her voice falters. She's unable to compartmentalize dinner or the assurance in my response. We hang up, so she can proceed to the test.

When I arrive home, I greet her at the bottom of the stairs with my coat and shoes still on, holding her coat expectantly, knowing we have reason to celebrate.

"We're pregnant!!!" She squeals with ecstatic joy as she bounds down to leap from the last step into my arms.

To commemorate the moment, we head to a franchised Italian restaurant and are seated at the bar to wait for a table. Evidently, hump-day is a big pasta night. I order a drink and Annie's favorite appetizer, coconut shrimp. *Wait, are pregnant women allowed to eat shrimp? I'd better read a book.*

We don't wait long, and I transport our order to our dining destination. The waitress unknowingly opens the door to our elation, "Are you guys celebrating anything this evening?"

"Why yes!" I pronounce leading Annie to blush. "We're pregnant!"

"Congratulations. How far along are you?"

Her interest does not seem piqued. She has probably had someone drop this tidbit on her before. I go for shock and awe. "We found out, oh," I look at an imaginary wristwatch, "about an hour ago. You're the first person we've told."

"Wow." She has to catch herself from stumbling while bringing her hand to her chest. She doesn't know how to continue the conversation, and the hanging silence makes her blush. "I'll give you guys a minute to check the menu."

Annie nudges my foot under the table, "Why did you have to freak out the young girl like that?"

I smile sheepishly. "We had to tell someone. We're not gonna be able to tell anyone else for ten to twelve weeks."

"Five to seven weeks," Annie corrects as she peruses her dining options.

"Is it safe to say that early?" I legitimately know nothing about the inner workings of the mind or body of the feminine persuasion.

"I'll be past the ten week mark then."

"Wait," my math must be a little off, "how will you be past the ten week mark?"

"Well, when was my last period?" She quizzes, smiling in a nurturing manner that lets me know she's about to softly teach me a lesson. This method makes me think she will be a great mother.

"It was supposed to be last week," I assert my counting skills.

"No, the last one I had." She reaches her hands across the table to tenderly cover mine.

"Five-ish weeks ago." A bewildered sense of dread begins to settle on me.

"You count from first day of your last period. So, we are five weeks pregnant," she beams reassuringly holding me in her eyes.

"So, we only have 35 weeks left?" I pull at my collar; *I thought I had the full 40.* The encroaching reality is making me flush.

"Yes, dear." She supports me as the weight of what's going to happen comes to rest firmly on my shoulders.

"I better get my act together." I glassily stare off into nowhere.

Day 75

I want to scream the news from the rafters, but alas, I can't. We're not supposed to reveal until ten to twelve weeks have passed and the baby is more viable. It was a bit of a shock that Annie's already five weeks pregnant. That lesson must have passed me by in health class. It's troublesome the five extra weeks I thought I had to transform into a father have been stolen. I make my peace with the fact that we only have to keep veiled for five more weeks.

I float through first period, but a disturbingly foul-mouthed youth brings me down from my cloud during second block. "If I see Ms. Wallace in the world, I'ma stick my dick in her mouth. I'ma feelin to get out fuckin bitches in the mouth, in the ass, in the pussy. Fuckin them young bitches, fourteen, fresh outta eighth grade. Could see me and Masters running a train on these hoes."

My attempts to curtail this adolescent's rant have fallen on deaf ears because the escalation has achieved the desired audience and applause. I increase my proximity to young Helmsley and place a hand on his shoulder to interrupt his momentum. He shrugs it off. "Don't touch me!" he growls and continues to describe how he has young ladies gargle his seed.

"Mr. Helmsley, can I have a moment with you outside?" My hand rests firm on his shoulder this time. Mistake.

"I said don't fuckin touch me!" Helmsley vaults out of his chair and grabs my shirt in his two balled fists. Our noses are inches apart as we realize that neither one of us can back down. His peers want to see Helmsley clock a teacher, and they watch me carefully to see how I handle a brazen assault.

Calmly yet curtly, "You need to let go and sit down."

"I told you not to fuckin touch me," he tries to assert himself, but his eyes betray him.

"Sit Down!" I growl. There are no positive outcomes to this situation.

"Make me," he sneers, and as he turns to receive accolades for his courage, I swiftly shove him backwards and down into his seat.

He springs back up. "You wanna fight, bitch?" His forehead pushes against mine, and I hold the tension.

152

Attempting to cover myself and validate a physical altercation with a youth, "You were and are in my personal space in an aggressive manner. I had to remove you. Now, SIT DOWN!"

He blinks, "This bitchass motherfucker assaulted me. You all saw it." His finger spans the classroom. "I'm gonna have your bitch-ass fired." He places an accusatory finger inches from my nose, and I momentarily entertain the wild thought to bite his hand.

I use his baulk as an opportunity to retreat to my desk. Busying myself trying to write down a detailed timeline of events, I try to process through whether or not I was justified in laying hands on a student.

"Yeah, bitch!" Helmsley is kneeling on his chair to lean well beyond the end of the desk, sneering, "I'm gonna write a complaint on yo ass and get yo ass fire. Bye, bye," he waves me away.

"Mr. Helmsley, you need to step outside." I try to retake the reigns in a calculated manner.

"Fuck you, bitch! You can't do shit. I punked yo pussy ass." He reaches out to receive an affirmative hand slap from a peer.

Not wanting to further escalate the situation, I request assistance from the hallway guard. "Can you remove a youth for me?"

The guard enters without needing me to identify the problem. "Kane, this bitchass teacher assaulted me. On my momma he did."

Mr. Kane stoically ushers the young man out. "Step out, dawg."

"Fuck this cracker!" Helmsley uses two fingers to motion he is shooting me, blows off the barrel, and lets his tongue hang out tauntingly as he leaves.

The top of my head is numb and my arms tingle gelatinously as I continue to write the incident report. Pausing, I realize that if I turn this in, it validates Helmsley's claim that there was an altercation. If I come under scrutiny, I stand to be disciplined or fired for this. The union can't truly protect me until my probation ends, six months into employment.

Putting the referral into the lower drawer of my desk for safe keeping, I decide to sit on it to see if things blow over. Mr. Kane reenters on cue with his hand on the scruff of Helmsley neck. "Just have a seat and chill, dawg. If you don't disrupt, Masters ain't gonna bother you." Nodding to me, he takes his leave.

The next fifty minutes inch by precariously. Neither Helmsley nor I know how to treat the other, and we both guiltily feel we're in the wrong and could be disciplined for our actions.

Class change ushers a wave of relief. As I grade Helmsley's work, which looks like an elephant wrote it holding the pencil in his trunk, my confidence rests in the fact that Helmsley hasn't the intelligence, writing skills, or attention span to pursue a complaint against me. I may have dodged a bullet.

Day 77

A nervous yet confident sense of relief washed over me when I walked to my car on Friday. Mike's managerial style is to have a firm hold of a fire extinguisher and put out the closest blaze that threatens to get too hot. If something regarding my indiscretion hadn't come across his desk in 48 hours, I try to reassure myself that the weekend has washed away my sins.

I spoke too soon. "You're a little later than usual?" Mike begins the week by greeting me at the front gate. He sits nonchalantly, sipping some gas station coffee. I stand dripping on the floor, trying to manage my umbrella as my boss subtly chastises me.

"It's ten to eight. I'm on time . . . right?" I cautiously defend.

"Yeah, I just thought you usually get here earlier." Mike has an uncanny skill for using any and every opportunity to illustrate the reality that he has his boot firmly on my throat.

"Well yeah," I lie, "I usually get here at 7:40/7:45" (I haven't gotten here that early in a month) "The downpour hit me in the middle of town. People don't know how to drive in the rain."

"Hmmph," Mike thoughtfully sips, leaving me dangling.

My heart is still pounding when I reach my class. I thought for sure Mike was at the front gate to prevent my entry. There are horror stories of employees being confronted at the gate, being relieved of their ID and chit, and turned around never to be seen again. I think Mike likes to feed off that mythology much like an interrogator shines a light in someone's face to reveal the truth. Secrets eat at us. They want to come out.

"This is fuckin BULLSHIT!" Mrs. McDonough has arrived. "I take one M F'n day off, and I get written up!" McDonough brings her tumult into my room for counseling services. The doctor is in. "You watch yourself, Masters. He smiles through fangs, man. That shithead is a snake. A fat, choking-on-a-rat, snake!"

"What happened?" I figure I might as well curry favor by letting her blow off steam. I've gotten the gist of the story already.

"So, I call in on Friday because my daughter's sick. Before I can even make it back, this shit is waiting in my mailbox." She shoves a

155

letter at me. It looks very official with the state letterhead on top, and Mike's signature is at the bottom announcing the first disciplinary step in the attendance policy has been implemented.

"What does this mean?" I haven't yet had the opportunity to return from an illness only to feel worse than when I was sick.

"Nothing, really. He just likes to stick it to us at every turn. If I get two more of these in three months, then I can get disciplined. But, this ASSHOLE doesn't even wait until I get back to see if I have a doctor's note. Shoot first; you can always pull the slug out later." She droops back to her classroom, fuming, and mutters, "Shithead."

Day 80

Casey and I stare at each other from across a circle of tables we have set up in the school library for today's Strategic Behavior Systems meeting. We are ten minutes past the start time, and only Dr. French is in attendance. He glances at his watch, states to no one in particular, "I have work to do," gets up, and leaves.

Five minutes later, Ms. Brown relieves us. "Mike isn't coming. He has a meeting this morning with the warden and other higher ups."

"When did he find this out?" Casey makes no attempt to hide his ire.

"I don't know. He mentioned it to me yesterday on the walk to the gate," Ms. Brown confides.

We push the tables back to their original positions, and Casey airs his frustrations, "I'm getting really tired of this bullshit. I've been doing SBS for five years, and nobody takes it seriously because of shit like this. I mean, we have a real opportunity to make some needed changes around here. But instead, we are constantly blown off. How low of an opinion do you have to think of people to just blow them off like this?" What he wants to convey as indignant rage leaves Casey fraught on the edge of tears. "I know those two are butt buddies," channeling his angst on Lashonda and Mike, "but I really wish we'd get treated with some sort of decency."

The day is littered with a cacophony of 'kids say the darnedest things':

We begin with a rousing interruption during the first block of the day, "You can't go to college by sniffing gas to get high." Due to security concerns, only Madison House, or 'Madhouse' as it is fondly referred to because of its population of special treatment boys, is in attendance. Their favorite past time is to debate over who is more mentally ill. They wear the label of 'institutionalized' as a badge of honor, bragging about any and every facility they've attended. Bonus points if they were 'kicked out.'

"Yeah, you a hype," another instigator chimes in.

My poor, studious, dopey loner falls right into the trap, "What's a hype?"

"You a hype if you smell gas to get high," the first provocateur explains.

Aiming to detour the conversation, I add, "I didn't think people huffed anymore." I've found it more effective to divert rather than derail or attempt to hit the brakes.

"What is 'huffed?'" The lead instigator is easily distracted.

"Huffing is breathing stuff in to get high," I educate the youth. "It was only popular for a short time in the mid-90s because like one in three people died the first time they did it."

The boys ponder this fun fact as Dopey does not accept my diversion. "My mom got kicked in the teeth by a horse once."

Really? "What does that have to do with what we are talking about?" I'm baffled that this young man asking to be ridiculed.

"It happened when she was younger," he clarifies, "like in the nineties. Hey, can I use the bathroom to turn around my drawers? I think I put them on backwards."

Hopeless.

"Yo, yoyoyo, my name Little C and I'm here to say," a very small Hispanic kid leads the way into second period, hyping for his large black friend. He rapidly finishes his introduction, "Fatchopsdon'tgangbang, hedostains, callhimtwofiddycauseheblowyourbrains. OOOOHH!!!" The duo does a ceremonial handshake into half-hug and finds seats.

"Gentlemen," I attempt to turn down the energy, "can we enter class quietly? Without gang banging?"

The chirpy Chihuahua, Jorge Masgeval, continues to be the voice of the operation. "Masters, we don't gang bang. We rock steady. We fuck hoes and front moes. You know?"

"I don't. What was all that rapping about?" I'm cautious, yet curious. Jorge repeats his line at the same pace, if not faster. "Okay, if you want me to believe you, you have to slow it down, so human ears can comprehend it."

"Fat chops," pointing to his compadre, "that's my boy here. Fat chops don't gang bang," he pauses to allow it to sock in. "He do stains."

"What is a stain?" I shouldn't have asked.

"You know, what happens at the end." Jorge makes a thrusting motion as he walks me through an anatomy lesson. "Leaving that stuff in a girl can get her pregnant. Instead, Fat Chops pulls out and leaves a stain on her. You know, like marking his territory."

It can be disheartening, the generational degradation of women. I half hope our coming child is not a girl because I don't want to be in a future prison cell next to these clowns for the murder of some pubescent wannabe Casanova.

Jorge further expounds, "Fat Chops don't gang bang; he do stains. Call him Two Fiddy 'cause he blows your brains."

"Is Two Fiddy your street name?" I direct at the round cheeked lad.

Jorge retains his role as voice box of the people. "Nah Masters, he weighs two fifty. And when he goes at the end of fucking a hoe, it's so much so fast that it blows her brain out her head." He beams with pride over his clever lyricism. A worthy reason to burst their bubble escapes me, so I let them have this.

It makes my skin crawl to watch a crowd mercilessly pick on one kid. Having a history of being teased and bullied for being 'the fat kid,' these acts are a sore spot for me, and I feel compelled to defend the weak.

Two boys decide to target one of the quietest, mousiness, hardest working kids I've had so far. "Yo faggot! I heard you'll get on your knees for anybody." Snidely leaning closer, he waits for a retort. "You get good merch for your BJ's, faggot?"

"Man, I fuck bitches." My studious pupil waves them off.

A second hyena begins to circle. "You never fucked no hoes in your life. Yo virgin ass."

The first bites, "Yeah faggot, you a virgin!"

I can't help myself. "How can he be a faggot and a virgin? Is that even physically possible?"

The two scavengers startle from the noise as I continue. "I mean, if he is a faggot, doesn't he have to fuck a dude? How can he be a virgin faggot? Does that mean he just likes to whip it out and sword fight?" The aggressors shrink back in embarrassment, not sure how to retort. "And, how would you know he's a faggot virgin. Were you the one sword fighting with him? Or, do you just like to watch?" The original prey lightly shakes his head at my antics with a twinkle

159

in his eye. "Are you guys mad because he won't give you any sweet lovin? Good for you." I bolster my teacher's pet. "You're saving it for someone special."

The prey escapes smiling without looking back at the two hyenas are too dumbfounded to continue laughing.

Day 81

The earliest doctor's appointment Annie could get is today at 2:00. The upside is a half day Friday and the weekend to process this monumental confirmation. The down side: Mike signed off with raised eyebrows. It seems a foreign concept to him that a doctor would see patients on a Friday afternoon. Maybe he thinks they should be busy golfing.

I'm feeling a little anxious about the whole thing when Ms. Brown interrupts my second hour class. "Just a heads up, no school this afternoon."

Joyous news! Maybe I won't have to verify my appointment after all. I don't mind telling Mike we're expecting, but I've had a couple of friends who jumped the gun, lost the baby, and the follow up conversations left much to be desired. "Not that I would ever complain, but did anyone give a reason?"

"Yeah," Ms. Brown enlightens me, "the union's holding a rally and elbow-rubbing dinner in the capitol tonight. Anyone who has personal time is encouraged to go to get our back pay. We'll be less than half staffed in the school, and security looks to be an issue next shift." I'm not sure if it's wise to reveal coverage issues in front of inmates, but the agreed-upon consensus is the kids know pertinent information long before we do.

"Thanks for the heads up." This is a serendipitous coincidence that could ensure my privacy. "High Five Friday!" I cheerfully extend to Lashonda, who receives it tentatively, strongly indicating she is just humoring me.

Day 82

"Good news, sports fans!" Mike does not wait for Casey to call the meeting to order. Instead, he jumps out of his seat excitedly passing out Terrific Tokens to the gathered group. "I spoke with the warden on Thursday, and he gave us the go ahead to implement Strategic Behavior Systems for the whole facility. If things go well, we'll be a model for the whole state!" In his eagerness, he completely forgets to apologize for jilting us at the last meeting. "Starting tomorrow, all departments will be issued Terrific Tokens at the gate to be handed out to youth for outstanding actions. The youth or the staff can turn them in at the school for the weekly drawing."

"What if they don't go to school?" Youth Correctional Officer Kane speaks up to calmly level an objection. "Ya know; the graduates with jobs that keep them out of school. How are they rewarded or motivated?" Mike is immediately caught off-guard by a population he neglected.

While participation in the meetings is 'voluntary,' the chief of security has to order candidates like Kane to attend due to lack of interest. Security guards do not cohabitate well with others because it is their job to ensure the safety and wellbeing of everyone inside these walls. Meanwhile the rest of the staff circumvents these procedures undermining securities capabilities or treats them like janitors who mop up the mess after someone has set off a kid and walked away.

"We'll get them their treat." Mike waves off any validity of the objection to press on, "Everyone on grounds will be expected to have these on their person at all times, and it is suggested that each staff hands out five a day," pausing momentarily to let it saturate. "Any questions? Good." Mike abruptly sits and waves an open palm toward Casey to proceed with the regularly scheduled meeting.

"Mike, I have an SBS idea I would like to run by you." I wait in the doorway to be invited in.

Hearing the magic acronym, Mike beckons me to a chair. "Sit."

I close the door behind me. "I'm excited that SBS is going to spread beyond the school. I think if we can treat the whole kid, we'll

162

see some real change. And, I really like your idea to have everyone carry tokens. It focuses the mindset on finding the positives." I butter him up with compliments before teasing out my agenda. "I think we might be able to go even bigger. . ."

Giving pause to ensure I haven't overstepped, Mike opens the gate. "I'm listening."

"I think that our whole point system needs to be retooled. Right now, kids are given a certain number of points which they can 'lose' throughout the week. It is essentially a demerit system which is counteractive to the SBS principals," I break momentarily, allowing enough time for this thought to germinate, "Essentially, we need a system that reflects the professional world. You don't get a paycheck, and then your boss can take it away." Mike actually perks up at this thought. Continuing, "You earn it by showing up and doing your job."

Mike scratches his chin as he ponders. "I'm interested in your proposal. I think I would have to see what it looks like before we go any further."

I've hooked him! Realing it in, "Can I draw up a sample?"

"Yes. Have it to me before the next SBS meeting, and we'll see if it is worth sharing with the group." Shaking his hand because I assume that's what you do when granted an enticing opportunity, I vault the stairs, two-by-two, excitedly renewed and ready to take on the kids.

A fight in the dietary and the confusion of a last minute SBS meeting further delay the start of the academic day. The initiative isn't winning over many people when Mike gives such little notice to security to adjust the youth movement schedule. The rapport that he preaches he fails to achieve with any department, including his own.

I use the postponement to tell Casey the news. Not wanting to offend or overstep my role in the group but ready to burst with the possibilities of revolutionizing an entire institution, I have to let it out. My mind teases out the possibilities dreamily as I enter 203. *Could this lead to a consulting career or a college professorship?* "Casey, guess what?"

"No school!" He looks giddily hopeful, clenching his fists close to his mouth in wishful expectation.

163

"No, sorry." Letting him down isn't a good starting place. "I wanted to run by you that Mike gave me the go ahead to make a new point sheet prototype."

The words hang in the air as I measure his response. "Do what you want," Casey replies, very blasé.

His response isn't what I was expecting, but it's not the worst case either. "Is something wrong?" I push for understanding.

"Yeah! Those two piss me off! They gave me the responsibility to run SBS and then randomly drop bombs on me unannounced. I never got into this to parade SBS around the grounds. I participate solely for the school and my kids. Trying to spread SBS around grounds is too big a ball to tackle. I'm done with it." Exasperated, surrendering, "I'm telling Mike I quit."

Gently capitalizing on a secondary opportunity, "If you're fed up, I'd love to take it off your hands for a while, just to give you a break. I would keep you in the loop and would need your expertise along the way."

"Whatever," defeated, "it's your funeral. You'll see." Ramping up, "You haven't been around long enough. You don't understand this place." Realizing that anger directed at me is wasted, "Do what you want. You'll figure it out."

"Thanks." I quietly leave Casey with his internal struggle. Strong outward emotion has never sat well with me. Crying at funerals or other public displays of grief is a borderline phobia of mine. I can remember when I was a child and my dad took me to a baseball game; he jumped out of his seat with the crowd to cheer as I sat unaffected. Even now, I've never really gotten into that. I think I process emotion slower than other people and prefer to do it in private. Maybe I'm on the Autistic spectrum. Everybody has their quirks.

Unable to shake the excitement from my system, I utilize down times during the morning classes to doodle possibilities. There are two major factors to consider: a new system can't create more work for security, and it must have more of an accountability impact on the kids. The end result is a half-sheet point card that assesses kids' points at no more than two hour intervals. The card holds a week's worth of points, and kids will learn responsibility by having to carry it around. Allowing the boys to hold it creates teaching interaction with a multitude of staff and partially takes the burden of awarding points off security's' shoulders.

Before presenting it to Mike, I run the new sheet by Mr. Vincennes to get a security perspective. He likes how the overall idea of 'earning' rather than 'losing' points will reduce conflict. He also approves of giving youth charge of their sheets as a measure of self-discipline. "I like your gumption, Mr. Masters. I think this place could use a shakeup, and you seem to have some life in you. I'll warn you, change is a slow, difficult process. If you are going to go through with this, be ready to climb a steep mountain covered in ice. Even if you backslide, find a different path and keep going."

"Thanks for the vote of confidence." The look of excitement in this weathered man's eyes energizes me. He really believes in me, and I respect him, so I'm further motivated to not disappoint him.

"My only critique: what if the youth throw out their sheet?" Vincennes poses a predicament I'd already solved.

"Great question. The privilege levels and incentives will be based on these sheets, so those will naturally motivate the youth to value the sheets. Also, the parole board is leaning toward not allowing bronze level kids to be released. So, that will make these sheets golden," I shamelessly pun.

"What about bullying?" He persists but not to derail. "What if someone gets bullied into giving up his sheet to be forged by a peer?" He's peppering me with devil's advocacy questions to prep me for the climb.

"That'll need to be handled on a case-by-case basis. The security will keep track of days earned toward level advancement, and if it is truly a case of bullying, we'll allow the student to continue from the interruption place without penalty." This makes Vincennes smile. I can think on my feet, and his confidence bolsters me.

My last stop before returning to Mike's office is Lashonda Brown. Mike operates with no real backbone of his own. Instead, Lashonda holds the clout to pull the plug at any point for any reason. I lay the proposal in front of her in homage. She tries to mask her approval but gives away a slight glint. "This might work. Good luck presenting it to security. They'll be your biggest critics."

"So, I have your blessing to present it to the committee? I know SBS was originally your baby, and I don't want to come off as overstepping my place in line." Waiting expectantly, her response won't stop me, but I stand to make a mortal enemy without her approval.

"You don't need a blessing; you need a miracle. Security will eat you alive, but it should be entertaining to watch." Smiling slyly, she is jealous that she didn't rewrite the point system first, but she isn't petty enough to block my ambitions.

"Do you see anything that I should tweak before bringing it to Mike?" I subordinate myself one more time.

"Nope. Good luck." Her well-wishing feels more like being shoved into a lion's den, but I'm confident I've covered my bases and will soldier on.

Mike's stoic thoughtfulness conceals his lack of any real cognition. He nods at appropriate points as I blaze through a bunch of social-psychological jargon that he doesn't register. I innumerate the concerns Security Supervisor Vincennes exposed, and Mike seems to be happy with my rebuttals. There are only precious minutes left in lunch, and I unwisely try to squeeze all this in before afternoon school. I hope my zealousness doesn't hurt my chances.

Pausing to ponder, or because he hasn't quite realized I'm done, Mike swallows a bite of his sandwich and pronounces his verdict. "Mindy Paulsen, our SBS consultant from Upper State University, will be here in a couple of weeks. I'd like you to present this to her at the committee meeting. If you get the approval from the committee, I'll take it to the leadership meeting later that day."

Trying not to explode from the excitement, I vigorously shake Mike's hand once again and bound back to my room, unable to shake a surging jolt of joy. My life's purpose has been to service the students no one else could reach. And now, I have a platform that could exponentially multiply my passion and influence. I'm realizing a dream I didn't even know existed, and I hope this feeling never fades.

Nothing gold can stay. My idyllic hangover reaches its painful peak as the last students are excused for dismissal. Expectant exuberance gives way to fear of the finicky, fickle staff. My self-image as a savior is popped by a peer group who fights against any current around every bend. If my ideas come anywhere close to being realized, it will probably be because I've been martyred along the way. Mike and Lashonda will pick up the pieces and get all the credit. My only hope is for gainful employment in the aftermath.

Day 85

"Masters, turn that honkey shit off before I beat your cracker ass!" Elias Presley objects to the Gospel music I softly play while the boys finish a worksheet. The positive message helps me counteract some of the negativity that constantly swirls around this place constantly.

"You're welcome to take your best shot," I retort.

"I would fuck your ass up," Elias sneers with contempt.

"Hey, hey, I know you haven't seen a girl in a while, but stay away from my ass." If I felt his threats held merit, I'd have chosen a different approach.

A little embarrassed, he feels he must escalate to save face. "Do you know who I am?" A fan-favorite for tough guys. Some Italian Mafioso said it in some gangster movie, and now every wannabe thinks he can trade off this tactic.

"No," I level. "And you don't know who I am."

His machismo begins to betray him. "What's that supposed to mean?"

I capitalize on the power shift. "Well, Mr. Presley, I've been doing this for eight years," leaning forward and brushing down both sides of my face to goad him, "and I don't have a scratch on me."

Seeming to shrivel a little, "Are you threatening me, Masters?"

Since his statement is slightly accusatory, I measure my next move carefully. "Not at all. I am a teacher. I'm just giving you a free lesson."

He smiles out the right side of his mouth, "You know, you alright, Masters. You still need to turn this shit off. It's giving me a headache."

Taking advantage of a teachable moment, "Presley, I thought the back of your ID says you are a Christian. You don't like Gospel music?"

Defensively, "Of course I do. Just not this white shit."

"This is a black artist," I defend.

"Nah, really?" I've got him all twisted in knots.

I set him up for a trap. "What would you have me listen to?"

"Turn it to 101.4, Hip Hop Hotlist." He doesn't bat an eye.

"You know hip hop music is probably the reason you're here?" I challenge his beliefs.

The conversation has transpired so far beyond his sphere of understanding that he seems committed to seeing where this is going, "How do ya figure that?"

"Well," a real learning opportunity has begun, "what are some of the points of discussion in hip hop."

Having lost the last couple of rounds, Elias refrains from making any offensive moves. Not wanting to give me further ammunition, he hangs back to see what I'll do next.

"From what I've listened to, violence, drug use and drunkenness, gangbanging, and gratuitous sex are what most of the songs are about."

"Not all of them," he attempts a defense.

"You're right. But, if you listen to hip hop long enough, that's probably the message you're gonna get," I challenge.

"So?" New ideas are working their way through his head.

I push the questioning to ingrain some wisdom. "What kind of jeans do you wear? What kind of shoes?"

Elias names several companies for which each item costs well over one hundred dollars.

"If you had your choice of alcoholic beverage right now, what would it be?"

He rattles off top shelf tequila, vodka, and cognac. *What seventeen-year-old drinks cognac?*

Icing the cake, "What kind of car will you be getting when you get out of here?"

Elias shoots for the stars and names a three hundred thousand dollar car I believe requires a chauffeur.

"Where do you think a kid from the inner city gets ideas about such luxury labels?" He knows I have him. "Modern rap music is just another billboard for overpriced products. The artists actually get paid to wear certain clothes and name certain brands. Most of what you see on the video is not actually theirs. How much do you think the typical rapper makes?"

He jumps at the chance to get back in the ring. "At least five or six million."

"I think that's an overestimate, but we'll run with it. After taxes and paying your agent, you can cut that in half. So, you have three mil. Now, you have to buy a house, a couple of cars, a chain, and a wardrobe. You're gonna party with an entourage every weekend. It won't be long before the funds run out; you'd be lucky to not owe money. So, you're twenty years old with no education but used to a glamorous lifestyle. What will you do?" I inquire.

The million dollar question stumps him. I enlighten the class. "This promise that quick money will solve your problems is a myth. The music industry wants you to fanaticize over it so they can keep selling records. But in the meantime, real people like you believe and hope for that opportunity to be a rapper or sports star and can't handle normal life when fortune doesn't fall in your lap. Getting a job and grinding out a living for fifty years is now made even more difficult because you expected riches to just fall in your lap. Then, you use drugs to cope or try to cut corners and break the law, ending up here."

The class is captivated. Elias attempts to lighten the tension. "You're doin too much, Masters. It's just music."

"You're right. It is 'just music.'" I pull back slightly to soften the delivery of the finish. "But, be aware of the message you're letting into your mind. I hear you sing it to yourselves as you walk the halls. You're not even aware you're being brainwashed." Turning the Gospel channel up, I leave them with one final thought to chew on, "Your mind, like your body, does better when filled with good things. Now, finish your work."

Day 87

Groggy teachers are corralled upon entry for an unscheduled early morning meeting. "Would you like me to start with the good news or the bad news?" Mike smiles in an attempt at levity. "First, there will be no school tomorrow." He pauses, and several teachers give him applause. "Instead, we will be moving." The stone-cold faces of the teachers indicate that if they could change their cheers to jeers, they would. "Now, it'll only be temporary. The internet people say that the wiring will only take six weeks, three for the upstairs and three for the downstairs. But on the bright side, we will have computers in the classrooms." Mike pumps his fist for good measure, but no one buys the enthusiasm.

"You said the internet people," Mrs. McDonough senses Mike is not being forthright. "What about the power? This place is already a fire hazard waiting to happen. Will that be upgraded as well?" McDonough teases out the question like a cat batting a mouse she's already holding by the tail.

Mike winces at being discovered. "Well, the power was bid out at three hundred and fifty thousand dollars." He cringes for emphasis. "The state accepted the bid but has not allocated the funding."

"So, why don't we wait and do it all together?" Casey has been visibly snippier since his perceived fall from grace.

"Because the state is ponying up the money for internet and you know we can't look that gift horse in the mouth." Mike chuckles at the state's reputation for not paying its bills.

"Why not wait 'til next week when we're doing report cards, so the boys don't miss school?" Mrs. Peters jumps on the wagon.

Mike rebuffs, "Either way, we'll have a week off while they are working upstairs. It actually works out pretty well." Mike nods to reassure himself.

"There aren't nearly enough classrooms for all of us," Ms. Vasquez, our robust art teacher, points out.

"Correct, Maria," Mike artificially praises. "You'll all be pairing up." He passes out a list of room and partner assignments. I've drawn the short straw with Mr. Tuck, but the positive is that we'll be

171

in a classroom and don't have to share the library. Perks of being paired with the seasoned crowd. "Use tomorrow morning to get with your co-teachers to formulate a plan. Conferences in the afternoon, and we start our new assignments Wednesday!" Mike claps as if to excite the group to action, but the teachers understand he's closing the book on any further discussion.

"So, Mr. Tuck," I chummily meander into his classroom and park atop a desk. "What do you want to do with all this?" Even though father time is younger and more coherent than Mr. Tuck, I offer him first crack at the planning of our new environment out of respect for his experience.

"Well, uh, Johnny," (no one calls me that) "uh, I think Mike has us teaching together." He must be on some sort of time lapse delay.

"Yes, indeed. Now, what would you like to do about that?" In vaguer terms, I restate the question, slightly slower and slightly louder, hoping for a more concrete response.

"Well." His attempt to clear his throat leads to a coughing fit, and he produces a handkerchief sporting several decades of decay. I think the cloth is possibly causing more problems than it is alleviating. Tuck composes himself but cannot regain his train of thought. "I guess we're supposed to be moving downstairs."

"That's right, sir," I reply, losing patience for this game. "I think I'm gonna make packets for my kids to work on. We'll only have three days until report card week. Would you like me to make extras for your kids?"

"Nah, nah, nah, nah . . . . . no need. I'll think of something."

"I'll see you in our new room, Mr. Tuck." I excuse myself to welcome entering youth and game plan this new wrinkle.

"See you there, Mr. Mazer. See you there." I don't bother correcting him. He's close enough.

Day 89

Just by serendipitous happenstance, the majority of our maximum security kids were released at the parole board yesterday. It makes the new teaching situation a little more palatable. In my excitement, I thought one of my favorites, Zion, would get to go home. Mrs. Grimly burst my bubble. "Sorry deary, he just went to court. Being a parole violator, he has to stay until his case is over, and he's facing some serious adult charges." She tries to sugar coat the outcome. "Likely, he'll take a plea and go to adult on a shortened sentence. If he fights his case, he'll remain here until the outcome." Ms. Brim crosses her fingers in hopeful emphasis. "Let's hope he stays a little while, and goes home on a win. "

The upside to teaching with Tuck is he has absolutely nothing to lose. Teaching more than half a century has left him a shell. Nobody will encourage him to retire because the change in routine will undoubtedly kill him, and no one wants that on their conscience. This new arrangement has thrown him for a loop. Tuck's struggle to adjust is well documented by Ms. Green who's had to escort him to our new room the past two days. At Tuck's suggestion, we show a "current events" movie for the first couple of days. That is how Tuck justifies showing the comedic portrayal of a black community organizer's accidental rise to the office of president. I know this lesson plan looks bad on my part, but I don't have the backbone to refute his choice. The problem with his illusive lucidity is I can't tell if he is bucking the system or legitimately thinks this is an appropriate civics lesson.

Antwon Bates holds firm to my attendance sheet. Despite our best attempts at intervention, Bates still refuses to complete any classwork. On the bright side, his disruptions and attempts to claim the title of 'Bull Looney' have lessened since our confinement conversation. If he decides to ramp up, I clearly and slowly express the expectations and proceed to ignore any and all of his coercive measures until Bates submits. Immediately praising his compliancy does not seem to register, but problems haven't persisted. We have a homeostasis established, and sometimes that's the best I can hope for.

Today, Bates has journeyed to his unresponsive, catatonic state before I have a chance to greet him. I'm acutely aware his mind is registering a completely different scene than what is present. Keeping the directives sparse, I pray he'll snap out of it. "Bates, please have a seat. We'll be watching a movie today." Due to his complete lack of any twitch or blink, I deduce Bates may be unaware I'm standing in front of him.

Not willing to shake him awake, I'm very thankful for the Youth Security Officer who trails Bates into the room to initiate intervention. "Yo Bates, what's shakin, man? I saw you walkin outta the gym. You look ready to kill someone." The guard astutely observes.

Bates vaguely responds to some sort of stimulus as he takes two more steps into the classroom but turns on an angle toward the whiteboard and away from the guard, stoically frozen like a centurion. "What's this guy's problem?" YCO Shade polls my pupils for insight.

A helpful youth who must be on Tuck's roster explains, "Somebody told Bates he's got no game as the bell was going off. Halfway here, he just kinda stopped in the middle of the hall. Hasn't said a thing since."

Bates seems stuck on a delay. He probably wants to respond to the insult, but the instigating youth is long gone. This apparent break from reality seems so severe it leaves me cautious to implement any interventions. I'm neither trained nor educated enough to bring him back.

Juvenile Supervisor Vincennes hears the commotion and takes immediate control. "Mr. Bates, find a seat." Unresponsive. "I'm going to ask you once more, Mr. Bates. Sit down!"

YCO Shade tries a softer approach as SS Vincennes unsheathes his shackles. "Come on, man. All you gotta do is sit through a movie. Then we bounce." YCO Shade emphasizes his friendly approach by placing his hand supportively on Bates' shoulder. Wrong move.

Bates perceives the touch as an act of aggression and whirls to shove Shade against the whiteboard so hard I swear Shade is lifted off his feet before crashing to the floor. Vincennes and another

Supervisor rush Bates and, with the help of Shade scrambling after Bates' knees, wrestle him to the ground. Three grown men have this youth pinched into the joint where the wall meets the floor. Bates bucks and roars, "Get off me! Get the fuck off me!" The commotion draws an additional two passing staff who take to the floor to further sandwich Bates.

The effort of five men is enough to get Bates handcuffed, but as soon as the pressure relents, Bates jumps to his feet and runs head first at the chest of the second Juvenile Supervisor, Chambers. The three guards lift Bates and run him out of the room, throwing him into the wall across from my room before returning him to the earth.

My attentions are drawn to keeping my assigned youth in their chairs whilst they crane for a better view of the action. "Nothing to see. Remain in your seats." My feeble first attempt doesn't convince them. "Anyone out of their seats will lose all their points!" gets their attention.

By the time I have the class settled, Bates has given up the fight. Being shackled is a tactical disadvantage, and Bates concedes; he is out-gunned. Before he closes me into the classroom, JS Vincennes instructs me to write up a disciplinary ticket and report documenting in detail everything I saw.

Turning to absorb the carnage of the six-man scuffle, two youth are pushing my desk back into place while another picks up my chair. Grateful to be showing a movie because crafting this narrative is going to take some time, I try to recount every detail to highlight Bates' illness and justify the use of force. My tale is almost complete when one of the students comments, "Hey, Bates is outside without a shirt on." *He was shackled in class with his shirt intact. How the hell did he lose it?*

Day 90

Gradually acclimating to another day, I busy myself with a morning ritual of making copies while scanning the latest addition of my attendance lists. Mike startles me. "Jon, your classes are going to be in the gym the next couple of days. We're doing GED testing in your room. Get to the hallway early to catch and redirect your youth."

I can't ascertain if this is because I'm the low man on the totem pole and all the other teachers don't want gym duty or because my class is in the corner and is a prime location for muted testing, but I don't buck it. The boys are going to be squirrely anyway because the quarter is ending. This time, the ever changing landscape adjusts in my favor.

Every kid is jubilated by the change in plans; not a one waits around long enough to hear an explanation.

Basketball is the sport of choice (mainly because it is the only equipment we've been provided) with half the court dedicated to a heated four-on-four game. The less athletic boys engage in a three point contest from the opposing corners of the court. I've coined the name "5-up" for the game because the point of the game is to go five shots ahead of the opponent for a victory. If the opposition does not hit the rim, the next shot is worth a double. Some games drag matching point for point, neither competitor able to make enough progress to end with a true win.

"Hey Masters," a cockily confident young lad chides. "I'll play you for a bag of hot chips."

"What do I get if I win?" I sweeten the pot.

Youth Jaine cannot fathom losing to a teacher. "I'll sit in the front row, do all my work, and get no referrals for the rest of the time here." He overplays his hand.

"How long you got?" I probe to get in his head. Half of the difficulty of this game is to have the attrition during the lead changes to pursue a victory.

"Two months," he boasts. This opportunity is too sweet to pass up.

176

"Deal!"

Five games later, I have as many students sitting in the front row, vowing to be models of scholastic performance. I joke with the guard on duty after my conquests. "It's only gambling if you have a *chance* at losing." I'll have to rearrange the class to fit more desks front and center. No way am I letting these kids welch. It's a teachable moment.

Day 91

Feeling under-the-weather today, I drag my feet back to the gym. I think the rusty ventilation circulating years of stale air is molding my lungs. Despite my infirmities, I add three more kids to the front row; two aren't even in my class. Having IOUs from inmates can't hurt. They track and honor those debts religiously. It's a thief's code or something.

"Masters, at some point it's no longer the front row." Mr. Frank criticizes my gamesmanship. We've cohabitated nicely. He's been relegated to the gym since the library has been repurposed as classroom space. "When they're all jammed together like that, they can move back en masse and tell you it's the new front row." He makes a valid point.

"That's why I draw little X's on the ground where the front corner of their desk needs to be," I craftily counter him. "Every young man is surprised when I point it out because I only enforce it when someone tries to pull a stunt. It keeps them accountable without having to power struggle. I make the mark with a wet erase pen, so when the room is cleaned, it vanishes."

Frank can't help but smirk and tip his cap. "Brilliant!"

During lunch, I survey my new, lower-level classroom to prep for afternoon school upon GED testing's completion. Sensing something amiss, I check my middle drawer, which has been left ajar, to find my reward candy isn't where I left it. I've fallen victim to a smash-and-grab job.

My afternoon classes are doubly indignant. First, they're surprised to learn they have to attend class when morning youth got to report to the gym. The knife twists when they find there'll be no candy. "What the fuck, Masters?"

"Don't blame me," I defend, holding up my hands. "Beat the kid's ass who took my bag."

Douglas, a newer edition to my roster, finds this amusing. "That was your candy?" he chuckles. "Parker was passing it out during group today."

"Dante Parker?" I troll for a positive I.D.

178

"Yep, that's the one." He persists snickering. "He sprung it on the intern lady leading group. Half-way in, he must have remembered he had it in his drawers. By the time that hottie tried to stop him, everybody'd had a piece. She yelled at us at the end of group to pick up all the papers."

Douglas wraps up his lark seeing I'm not amused. "Well, at least you got your reward," I feebly fume.

Trying to piece together the crime scene, I know Parker was in the gym second hour. He couldn't have had it on him then. He played basketball the whole period and left drenched. It dawns on me. Parker and Smits jetted down the back hallway before lining up. Smits must've seen the GED lady wheeling her cart out when he was returning from the bathroom, and they figured she'd have left the door open, having no keys.

Victimized, I figure, *what can I do?* My account of events is all circumstantial. I can't even be upset over a timely executed caper.

Day 92

Report card days are a contractual right, or so I've been told. Mr. Park, our union heavy hitter, instructs me, "Take your time, Masters. No prizes for first place. We fought long and hard to get this time, and when we're fully populated, it's really needed. Don't go rushin through and give Mike a reason to rethink the policy. It'll screw us in the back end."

"10-4." I show solidarity looking forward to a break. For a variety of reasons, the intensity of this population dictates they be in programming as much of the day as possible. Annals of files catalog what they're capable of doing with idol time. As for me, I've been involved in some form of year round school since my freshman year of high school. Not a summer has passed without attending or teaching summer school. My wife has tried to coax me to take a break, but I warn her, "You wouldn't like me with nothing to do. Sure, I might catch us up on some projects at the start, but after about a week, I'll lose the drive. With nothing to do, I'll do nothing. I'll wake up late, watch cartoons for hours while eating oversized bowls of cereal, and only shower if I can smell myself. I'll become a baseball fan only as an excuse to drink beer in the neighbor's garage. And, this cycle will continue for the duration of summer break."

Annie has since come around to supporting my dedication to education. Occasionally, I spring for a nice trip, and she has learned to appreciate having the house to herself over the summer. She's driven to accomplish the "honey-do" list in a way I never could.

Due to a complete lack of technology, the teachers are relegated to manual transcription. Hand-drafting report cards is brainless work. The trick is precision. We're allowed to use whiteout for minor mistakes, but too many errors can lead to a redo.

For students who have attended more than a quarter, I just have to copy the most recent report card with minor additions from this quarter. For those who haven't, the majority don't have records from other schools, so my finished product can be sparse. The emptier forms tend to lead to youth protesting about missing credits.

I probe Mr. Park as to whether I should use the time to track down transcripts, but he mirrors my tradesman uncle's sage advice. "Keep in mind, Mr. Masters, don't do well what you don't want to be stuck doing forever. Mike encourages proactive thinking like that and takes great joy in shouldering those thinkers with the burden of their idea. Anyways, that's part of Mike's job as principal. He's never gonna go out of his way to make our jobs easier, so we tend to return the favor."

Completing about 80% of my report cards before lunch, I decide it's time to stretch and take a walk. From a distance, I may look like a brown-noser, but being a procrastinator by nature, I counteract my innate tendencies by diving headlong into assigned projects right away. My organizational methodology embraces a piling, instead of filing, system. I'm fully aware that out of sight means out of mind, and I will soon forget what I'm supposed to do if it's in a cabinet. Being a little OCD helps too; I will ruminate on the stack until it dwindles and I can see my clean, cleared desk. If I finish early, I can always sit on the pile a while. At that point, I'll transport the stack closer to the door, so every time I come and go, I will consider ridding myself of the bundle. Regardless of when I finish today, I fully intend to follow the company line of turning them in late tomorrow.

As I loop around the hallways, I notice Julie Vargas eating a salad while perusing a novel. Ms. Vargas routinely reads through lunch solitarily, and I ask if I can join her today. "Do you mind the company? I won't disturb you," waving my own literature as proof. "I just need to get out of my class."

"Pull up a chair." She smiles and returns to her reading.

We sit in complete silence for the lion's share of our lunch break. It's surprisingly cathartic to enjoy someone else's company without using any words. "Same time tomorrow?" I inquire as I get up to leave.

"Yeah, that would be nice." Her kindness is a welcome port in this temperamental tempest.

After four and a half months, I have yet to settle in. I've been assigned to teach five different preps in four different locations. I feel incapable of getting any traction with my classes. Every time we've strung together a couple of weeks of school, some unforeseen

181

event dramatically changes the landscape, leaving us unable to continue on our current path. My rosters are shuffled enough to make a review or catchup impractical, and those who've remained are left unfulfilled due to the inability to continue from where they'd progressed. For the sanity of all, I resolve to assigning daily lessons and packets. This is not very challenging and builds to nowhere, but any attempt to do differently has resulted in the same outcome.

Even if I could maintain a consistent classroom, my gradebook illustrates consistency is unattainable. Reviewing the quarter's grades for my first period, I recall the first two weeks were taught on the houses. Week 3: Cameron, Franklyn, Jackson, Thompson, and Watkins were assigned to my class, though Jackson missed two days due to confinement. Week 4: Cameron, Franklyn, Jackson, and Neebel. Week 5: Jackson, Lorenzo, Neebel, and Xander; Cameron was moved to my fourth hour class without warning or explanation. Since once a week we have no afternoon school to leave room for house conferences with each youth's clinical team, I scrambled to find two days of packets for Cameron to do while the rest of the class caught up to him. Week 6 was spent attending Correctional Orientation Training at Southern State Penitentiary. My kids resided in the library, blatantly choosing to ignore my assignments. Week 7: Browning, Jackson, Jefferson, Lorenzo, Neebel, and Watkins. Evidently, Watkins requested another class that didn't work out. The grass was greener in my classroom, and Mr. Hicks was happy to accommodate Watkins's shifting moods. Week 8: Browning, Jackson, Jefferson, Lorenzo, Watkins, and Xander. Week 9 and 10 remained steady with Browning, Jefferson, Lorenzo, Page, Watkins, and Xander. But, last week we moved downstairs and doubled up teachers leaving me to finish with Browning, Lorenzo, Page, and Watkins. Not one of these young men was assigned to the same class for the entire quarter, nor did any youth receive schooling with any consistency. Our credit system is set up to award credit faster, but in truth, we can't keep pace.

Repealing any judgment against teachers I perceived as lethargic for passing out individualized packets and creating a glorified tutoring room, I press Julie Vargas for a thoughtful answer. "Is the school always this out of whack? How do you get used to the inconsistency?"

"It is a wacky place, but you'll get used to it," Julie encourages as she marks her place in the book. "It can be unnerving at the start, but you'll find your peace. We probably work less than 32 hours a week when you factor in lunch, breaks, and the walks to and from the gate. We can't come early or stay late or bring materials home due to security concerns. So, do what you can while you're here, but don't be a hero or a martyr. Don't overextend yourself and get burnt out. No one is checking up on us or asking us to do more. The plight of these kids is well documented. If you can keep most of your kids in your class for most of the period, you'll be a rampant success."

Thanking her for the wisdom, "It was serene reading in here. We should start the Lunch Munch Book Bunch. Make it a regular thing."

"About that. . ." She bites her lip digressing from her cheerful spirit. "I'll be leaving on Monday."

"What? You're joking? How come?" There are no footholds to be had in this place. Any time I think I'm secure, the grip fails, leaving me in a constant scramble.

"Keep it hush, hush," Julie warns with a finger to her lips. "I'm not telling Mike until Friday. I've had a transfer request in to adult for two years, and I won't give him a chance to mess it up."

The value of her advice has plummeted as I realize they are parting words. "Won't you get in trouble for the short notice?"

"I only found out on Thursday after work. I'll still be working for state corrections. I've just been reassigned." Julie is uncharacteristically conniving and mean spirited about the news. "Mike has taken great pleasure in disregarding any and every idea we've had to improve this place. He continues to drive it deeper into the abyss, and for that, I don't owe him anything."

This is a side of Ms. Vargas I wanted to believe couldn't exist. My perception of her purity gave me hope that someone could navigate this place unscathed. Instead, even Julie has become defensively aggressive, trying to vindicate herself and others the institution has scorned. Deep down she struggles with the knowledge that not giving notice is wrong but has convinced herself she is doing it for the right reasons.

"Good luck," I half-heartedly well-wish her. Unable to grapple with losing a mentor / role model / friend so soon, I bid her farewell. "You will be missed," I concede with a theatrical bow.

Excusing myself to process this news, my chest tightens as I enter my classroom. The pedestal on which I placed Mr. Sawyer and Ms. Vargas has cracked at its foundation and is crumbling. Realizing with a growing lump in my throat that no one has presented a healthy coping mechanism to overcome the evils of this place, I disintegrate into my desk and stare at the stacks. There is no hope of escape.

Day 93

Not being able to hold out any longer, I submit my report cards at one o'clock. My confidence betrays me as I can't remember Mike referencing the time frame during which he wanted them finished. Quietly hoping my coworker hasn't set me up for a cruel hazing ritual, I leave them in Mike's mailbox and scuttle back to my assigned area with nothing pressing to accomplish.

Juvenile Supervisor Vincennes provides a much needed distraction. Allowing time for him to wrap up his phone conversation, I perch just outside the security office doorway. "What can I do for you, Mr. Masters?" He greets me as he returns the phone to the receiver.

"Inquiring minds need to know. Can you tell me what happened with Bates?" I give him a sly smile and a knowing nod.

"I haven't the slightest idea what you're talking about," Vincennes returns my coy smile, unsure what to make of me.

"Don't worry. I wrote it up by the book. It was absolutely necessary to use force," I reassure him while revealing my suspicions. "But, I do remember Bates leaving my classroom with a shirt on. My kids noticed he got in a van without one. Now, how could that happen while he was cuffed?" I rub my chin for emphasis.

Vincennes leans forward to ensure the glass-framed office keeps our secrets. "Between you, me, and these walls, Bates did leave your class with a shirt on." Vincennes' eyes shift to indicate this will be juicy. "After Chambers had him cuffed, Bates got mouthy. Chambers was escorting him outside when Bates said, 'Get your hands off me, bitch.' Since Bates wasn't paying attention, Chambers walked him into the doorframe." I can't help but snigger at the visual.

"After recovering, Bates realized Chambers did it on purpose and kept going, 'Why'd you do that, bitch?' Chambers wrung Bates by the collar and pushed him against a wall saying, 'Call me a bitch again!' After a brief stare down, Chambers relented saying, 'That's what I thought.' I figured that was the end of it, but Bates never learns. He started into Chambers again, 'If you ever touch me again, you pussy ass motha . . .' Chambers interrupted him with a slam to the floor and put a knee into Bates's back screaming, 'I'm nobody's bitch, you piece of shit. Nobody's!'

"I had to pull him off and give him space to cool down. Bates got to his feet, and his shirt was nearly ripped in two. I ushered Bates into our office to cut the sleeves and slide it off." No longer smiling, he looks me dead in the eye, "If anyone asks, you're mum to this whole thing."

"What thing?" I reassure him playing dumb. It's exhilarating to be baptized into the security inner circle.

"Chambers could lose his job or worse for a small lapse in judgment," Vincennes impresses. We leave the moment hang in a morally gray area before Vincennes propels the conversation forward. "When's that point sheet presentation of yours."

"Thursday morning."

"I'll be there," he reassures. "I've seen how this place shoots down good ideas, and I want to help push this one through."

Emboldened by an ally, I feel confident that our conviction is strong enough to rise above petty workplace politics.

Day 95

Mike catches up to me halfway to the school. "You ready to present your point sheet?"

Being on the younger side and new to this institution, my confidence can easily be mistaken as cockiness. I choose a measured, humble approach. "I'm excited to hear suggestions. What I have so far is just an idea. It'll take the input from the group and some fine tuning to turn it into something we can all work with."

"Very good," Mike affirms my approach. "Also, I need you to draw up an itinerary for the meeting. I'm gonna make you the new SBS point person."

Taken aback by the sudden promotion of responsibilities, I muster, "Sure! No problem."

Given a couple hundred more feet for the afterglow to fade, I come to the uncomfortable realization that I've just usurped Casey's role. "Did Mr. Sawyer step down?" I ask to gauge how to navigate the potentially delicate situation.

"His heart hasn't been in it for a while," Mike astutely shares. "I think it's time for a break. I'll tell him this morning."

I'm dumbstruck by the flippancy with which Mike writes off one of his most dedicated teachers. As we enter the school, I initiate our parting with, "When should I be ready for the meeting?"

"Mindy Paulsen should be arriving at nine. Let's meet in the lounge," Mike instructs and disappears into the office.

Seeing Casey's classroom illuminated, I choose the long way around to avoid any awkwardness. There is no good way to tackle that conversation, and I don't want him to find out I knew about his demotion before he did and didn't give him a heads-up.

Searching my files to locate a copy of an old SBS committee schedule and then sneaking down the back stairs, I make it to the communal computer just in time to see Casey enter Mike's office. Casey finds a comfortable seat before standing again to shut the door. The meeting is surprisingly short, and I duck behind filing cabinets to hide my snooping.

187

Copying Casey's format verbatim, I sandwich my presentation between the Time Out Ticket report of Mrs. Wells and the discussion of which character traits should be highlighted next month, spearheaded by Ms. Brown. After wishing Ms. Erickson, our office assistant, a wonderful morning, I collect my copies and head for a quiet place to prepare myself for the coming adventure.

Unable to holster my nosey nature, I make a quick stop to check on Casey. "How you holding up?"

"Fine, you?" Casey glosses over the recent happening leaving me unable to tell how he's truly been affected by the turn of events.

"I wanted to apologize. Mike just kind of sprung this on me during the walk up. I never asked for this." I try to compartmentalize my excitement in an attempt at genuine remorse, but upon further examination, I feel I have no reason to be contrite. Casey legitimately didn't want to be a part of SBS anymore. He wouldn't relinquish the role because he wanted the experience as a feather on his resume.

"No worries. We're cool. You get to be Mike's prize pony now, so enjoy the ride." He seems to take pity on me. I think Casey sees a mirror of his own tenacity in me. He doesn't wish to burden anyone else with the weight he's been carrying, but I've pulled it down on my own head. Am I the fool? Only time will tell.

After a round of introductions, complete with trumped up title sharing, Mike disregards the agenda I handed out and instructs me to share my prototype. Scurrying around the table to hand out fifteen individual copies, I get off to a bumpy start. I instruct, "Just take a moment to survey the proposed new point card. I'll give you a minute to take it in and then give a short overview. I welcome any questions or comments."

Finishing, I overhear Mr. Davis, a security staff, mumble loud enough for most to catch, "You've got to be kidding." Immediate dissension does not make for a great beginning, but Mr. Vincennes comes to my defense with a grunt and a glare to shame the interruption. The silence is tense as everyone surveys the material.

Taking a deep breath, I proceed, "During the last meeting, Mr. Hicks shared that it is Warden Pritz's intention to spread Strategic Behavior Solutions throughout the institution." I share the blame, so the heat doesn't fall solely on me. "Having a background with multiple behavior systems, I thought a good place to start is our point structure. Right now, the youth get points twice a day and can have them taken if they don't comply. This essentially is a negative demerit system. It leaves little room for teaching interaction and instead creates combative positions for staff as they try to enforce policies."

Leaving a moment for this to sink in, I notice our SBS consultant, Mindy Paulsen, smiling and nodding encouragement as I continue. "Our current model is the opposite of SBS. In front of you is a proposal for a shrunken down version of the current weekly point sheet. I've broken up the time increments to allow the boys to 'earn' points at more intervals throughout the day." I emphasize the importance of semantics with air quotes. "This way if a young man has a rough spot in the day, it doesn't ruin his whole day, which may prevent him from giving up for long periods or days at a time."

Surveying the room, I perceive the audience as combative, so I pause to field questions and put out fires. A balding, middle-aged counselor named Mr. Schnell starts. "So how will the levels system work?"

"Thank you for asking." He's seamlessly transitioned to my next point. "I propose, instead of our week-by-week current system, youth would have to earn 80% of their points five days straight to go from bronze to silver. To go from silver to gold, they would need ten days at 90%. These are just figures off the top of my head. We can determine day and percentage requirements based on whatever the group agrees to. That can be subject to change, now or later, depending on the stringency we wish to convey."

The counselor continues, "Could they skip from bronze to gold?"

"No," I assert. "The key is the delayed gratification to rise from level to level. Under our current system, kids weekly bounce up and down multiple levels. The gold level currently means that a youth had one good week. The same youth could have just come off of five horrible weeks and return to such behavior once his commissary is ordered. Restructuring the transition of levels and connecting advances to incrementally higher achievement will bolster their meaning and value."

"How are we supposed to input these levels into our tracking system?" The counselor persists his an attempt to stump me.

I'm not familiar with this process. "How do you do it now?" Strategic Behavior Systems is a communal cooperative organism. I knew going in I wouldn't have all the answers. Organically, the counselor has a chance to be a part of the developmental process.

"The counselors input the levels on Mondays in preparation for Tuesday's conferences, so we can tell youth which level they are on." The counselor sits back, crossing his arms, feeling victorious for trapping me.

"Doesn't security know what level each youth is on by the end of the weekend?" I illicit a curious cock-of-the-head from the counselor. He won't affirm my claim but can't dispute it. "My kids come in beaming on Monday mornings bragging about their level. Does security tell them their level before conferences?" Pausing to leave an opening for protest, I continue unchallenged. "Why can't security tell a kid any other day of the week? Counselors can still input on Mondays if they like, and the boys can have more immediate gratification which is shown to be the most effective in changing behavior."

Soaking in my victory, I'm emboldened to take on all comers. Mr. Kane's cool, collected demeanor takes the next shot. "This looks like a lot more work than our current system. Who's gonna add up all these points?"

"Very good point, Mr. Kane. I think the youth should." The room shifts uncomfortably in tandem. I can tell no one likes this idea. "Hear me out. This will get the youth to be more aware and invested in the points they are earning. Security can spot check overnight, or whenever they normally add up points, to verify correctness."

"Sounds like a lot of work," levels Mr. Kane.

"I tried to keep it the same amount of work or less for all involved. Since the kids carry it around and are responsible for the sheets, security has to update them less often. The totaling is the kids' job, so hopefully security is spending the same or less time calculating the totals."

My rationale is not enough to appease Mr. Kane, but he will wait to monitor the rest of the group's reaction. Davis jumps at the opportunity to poke a hole. "What if the kids are caught forging the sheets?"

"Well, points should only be reported in pen." I smile showing I'm well aware of the boys' propensity to pilfer pens and markers. "Each point box has space for initials. If you believe the young man is forging, check with the staff who signed. If you can verify it, write a forgery ticket and the youth will have to start over and/or go down a level due to the ticket."

"That is definitely more work." Davis feels vindicated, snidely sneering, "Security is not going to agree to all that paperwork."

"Any change in programming is going to have an adjustment period," I counter. "Will some kids forge it? Yes. But, that doesn't mean you can throw out the whole idea. Think of the structure, discipline, and responsibility it will teach the youth and how that will change the climate of the institution. This is a tough job. If we can create a more motivated, disciplined clientele, it will make life more enjoyable for all involved."

Davis isn't backing down but isn't piping up either. "What happens if a youth refuses to carry the sheet or loses it?" Mindy Paulsen lobs a concern at me, intrigued as to how I'll field it.

"Mr. Vincennes gave me the idea." I pick up an ID clip that I brought to illustrate this point. "The youth can fold their point sheet in half or quarters and pinch it to their shirt with their ID. This also insures that youth are wearing their ID, which is a dilemma as well." I swell with pride after killing two birds.

"If the kids are carrying these around, they're gonna get tattered," Mr. Kane points out. "By the end of the week, they'll be in shambles, and quite frankly, I don't want to touch them if kids are going to be putting them in their shoe when they don't have an ID."

The validity of his point makes me backpedal. "What if the boys just carry it when they aren't with their security staff?" I offer. "They could use it like a pass when they go to school, or to a counselor, or a job."

"That still leaves them pretty beat up at week's end," Mr. Kane endures. He's not oppositional. Instead, he wants to solve a real problem. "And how will security collect and hold them all?"

"How do they do it now?" I recycle tactics.

"In a binder that stays on the house. Most CO's aren't gonna be too keen on the idea of carrying around 30 something sheets of loose paper."

Kane's got me flummoxed.   Leaving too much unanswered space, Mindy Paulsen jumps in. "What if we put all the kids on one sheet?" She pauses to observe security. Davis seems ambivalent, but Kane is willing to hear her out. "You can use Mr. Masters' chunking for the timeframes. Instead of having the youth carry it, security can hold one sheet on a clipboard. At the end of the day, another single sheet can hold the weekly running total, and," turning to the counselor, "the seven daily sheets can be turned in with the totaled weekly sheet to determine the grade."

"That would be less paperwork," the counselor admits. "Would we still do the five day, ten day level thing?"

"Let's shelf that for now." Paulsen has the podium and some gusto.   "I think we should restructure the levels, but this can be progressive. Rome wasn't built in a day." She makes a flirty wink to get the boys on her side.

"Jon, is it?" turning to me. "Can you draw up an example listing all the kids down one side with the same increments that you have now?"

I'm a little put off that my idea was so quickly tossed aside. I want to argue its merits more, but I settle for just staying involved. We have made progress.   "I'd be happy to," I relent. My pride's wounded, but I'm not certain where the inquisition would have taken us if she hadn't quickly saved it.

"Great! I think y'all have a lot to chew on before your next committee meeting.   Keep the discussion and ideas flowing." Paulsen cheerfully dismisses a meeting she has no authority over and pulls Mike aside. The remainder of the itinerary is disregarded, and I'm privy to why Casey's had so much angst over these meetings. Mrs. Wells and Ms. Brown collect the materials they prepared to share and quietly leave, slightly dejected.

Collecting my things, I resign to engineering someone else's vision.   I comfort myself with the thought that I can use the additional samples in my portfolio as examples of ingenuity and willingness to collaborate.

Mike halts my exit. "Mr. Masters, we would like you to join us at the SBS Leadership meeting to present our ideas to the Warden." Mindy Paulsen smiles reassuringly in the background, revealing this to be her idea.

I'm back in the game! These meetings are compartmentalized to obstinately reinforce the chain-of-command.   In a pure SBS environment, the Warden and anyone else involved should cohabitate with the lay people, including parent liaisons. As a power play, the warden doesn't show up to the 'committee' meetings, which dilutes the whole process. Recovering some optimism, I've just been called up to the Show on my first day as SBS point person.

As Mike and Mindy walk me immediately out the door leading the way to the administration building, I haven't the foggiest idea how or what I'm going to present. My original idea is in shambles, and frankly, my pride was too tarnished to recall all the tweaks made by Mindy. *What the hell*, I'll take a shot at my original plan and see if I can impress the Warden.

Ms. Paulsen earns her keep as she counters me point-by-point. Since the Warden doesn't know we are diametrically opposed, our duet appears deliberate. Warden Pritz rubber stamps his approval without really understanding much of what it entails, and I'm left with the task of reconciling the myriad of proposed ideas into a workable solution.

"Man! I forgot my sweater. I'm gonna freeze my butt off. This day already sucks!" Casey's on a rant before we reach the school.

"I'm not much of a cold weather person either. Making this walk in January is going to be treacherous."

"You have no idea. Make sure you have a good pair of boots because they don't shovel," Casey advises. "Also, get familiar with the location of the sidewalks. I walked over a half-wall and fell ass-deep into a drift. I mean, why don't they get the farm boys out here to shovel?"

"We still have a farm program?" I'm puzzled by his idiom.

"Well, not really," he recants. "That's what they call the guys who run the mowers."

"It would be awesome to teach these kids to plow and tend a couple plots in a field. Why don't we start that back up?" I share my idyllic musings.

"No teachers," Casey reveals.

"Come on, it's not hard to teach. Take a shovel, turn that soil over, poke it into small chunks, and repeat."

Casey expounds by enumerating the intricacies of our facilities shortcomings. "The problem is juvenile facilities are understaffed all around. We don't even have a YCO to spare for that kind of stuff. They do have programs like that in the adult pop. One facility to the north is nearly self-sufficient. All the crops grown are used in the mess hall. Other facilities have graduate programs."

"You mean to earn a bachelors?" It comes as a surprise that our state has funding for such entitlements.

"Yeah, they have that, but they've also started offering masters programs to equip the inmates for work beyond the facility."

"All free?" I'm unable to wrap my head around the fact that convicted felons get beyond a four-year education on the state's dime.

"Yup." His acceptance of how the machine runs is unnerving. "As for us, we're really short of programs here, and we're not prepping them well for reassimilation. I mean, we prep them in the school, but most of these kids aren't welcome back to the school

194

they should attend when not incarcerated. If they're caught dealing or have a weapons charge, schools tend to not want them back. If they go to alternative schools, they're around the same influences that got them here. I had one kid who was real sharp. He got out, but his school refused to take him and offered no alternative placement. The school had no obligation to take him because the kid's 17. Now, he's back. He got violated because part of his probation required him to pursue a high school diploma. Catch 22."

"I'm surprised a public defender didn't sink his teeth in that one. Any lawyer could've had their picture in the paper. Make a career out of it." I try to soften Casey's trauma over systematic iniquities.

"Nope. Nobody cares about these kids. They're just thrown away."

We've returned to teaching in pairs on the lower level. Tuck and I are the last ones privy to the new plan our colleagues concocted. Because class sizes are so small, most teachers have been alternating one teacher to instruct in the mornings and the other in the afternoon. The classrooms aren't conducive to dividing and conquering, and co-teaching is an art that takes time to master, but switching teachers saves time for everyone, they contend. The teacher not presiding over the youth stakes out in a classroom upstairs 'looking busy,' and Mike hasn't found a good reason to burst the bubble.

Guilt cripples me from jumping aboard. I can't picture letting Tuck fumble around, left to his own devices. I'm aware he was previously accountable for his own classroom, but now that we're teamed up, I feel responsible for him. I make peace with getting Tuck's class settled in and then taking off.

My plan hits a skid as one of my favorites shows no signs of slowing as he blows by class. Upstairs he could take an extra lap, but the hallway down here leads to nowhere. I follow Lucas to a dead-end corridor. Readying myself for anything, I'm caught off guard by what happens. He appears to be a breaking down and balling. "Let's talk over here," I offer as his waterworks start flowing. We sit in a row of bolted down chairs, and I put a conciliatory hand on his shoulder.

He is strong like only a body at the height of pubescence can be as he heaves uncontrollably. "These kids be testing me, Masters," he blubbers. "Guys be jawin and fartin in group. I try to move, but

195

'nother prick's touchin my head. Kids get three or four warnings, but first chance, I be gettin sent to my room."

Lucas takes a respite from sharing to sob. Looking back to me desperately, he confides, "I just said, 'I'm tired of this shit,' and the guards be like, 'stop all that talking. I'm gonna open your door. You run out and do what you do. Do what you gotta do.' I got a baby on the way, Masters. I'm tryin to get outta here." Lucas reveals his desperate inability to succeed given the current constraints. "I try to make gold level because I get a phone call. My mom can't come out here, and I haven't talked to my baby momma in a month. All I heard was that she healthy. My momma told me."

I'm dumbstruck as I try to relieve this kid's misery. "How old is your kid?"

"My girl's three months pregnant." He heaves between sobs.

That gives him six months. "How long you got left in here?" I prod.

"Eight weeks." He sniffles and attempts a wavery, cleansing breath.

"That gives you plenty of time," I comfort and reassure. "Stay on your square and ignore the fools. You've got bigger things to work for."

"I know." Lucas is not encouraged by the party line. "It's just getting so hard. This CO keeps buggin me. I can't shake 'im."

"Do you have grievance forms?" I offer. Finding it beyond belief that a youth corrections officer would feel the need to poke this kid, I feel no remorse over throwing a colleague to the wolves if he has beleaguered Lucas.

"I'm feelin to write one." Lucus snorts away the tears.

As he looks at me with courage, I make an effort to reinforce his will. "Good! Just avoid that CO and write the grievance when his shift is over. Don't be combative because you'll lose."

"Yeah, you right." Lucas attempts to stand, but I implore him to collect himself before he enters class. These scavengers will pounce on any perceived weakness.

Gaining composure, Lucas musters a half-heart smile. "Thanks, Mr. Masters. I'm all good." He shuffles to class. With a pause before the doorway, he fortifies his posture and enters the classroom with confidence.

196

Day 99

I spend my morning shower time ruminating on how to deal with the candy culprits. I've already promised the afternoon lot (because they are from another housing unit) I will continue to bring them candy for "Hard Work Hump Day," so I have to follow through for them. But, there's an unsettled feeling in my stomach over the proper way to address the pilfering.

Theorizing that coming off like a victim will lead these kids to run wild (empathy is not high on their list of character traits), while acknowledging anger hasn't worked for any school administrators, cops, or judges who've threatened them with all kinds of treachery, I stand by my conviction to let natural consequences take their hold. Since I can confirm the culprits are from 2nd period, I'll explain to that class, "Sorry, candy's gone. Most likely you either got some, or know who know it, or both. With that said, no candy this week."

As they protest, I'll work in a teachable moment. "Hey, hey! Don't blame me. Blame the thieves that ruined it for everyone," and they will. It might even guilt my sticky-fingered bandits into thinking twice before trying again. Doubtful.

Charles Willis glides into fifth period. Willis is a short yet sharp looking young man. The unstoppable charisma and confidence he exudes make it plain to see how much his momma loves him. This type of personality has a tendency to grind on me because, frankly, I think these kids should be a little more contrite. A brand new #2 pencil balanced on his ear enhances his bravado.

Pencils are a big source of contention because of the administration apprehension that they can be used as weapons. The youth protest that usable equipment is not available on the houses, and they need writing supplies to pen letters to loved ones. I'm able to find a happy medium by keeping religious track of my own supply and having a 'don't ask, don't tell' policy for students who behave.

Something about the way Willis carries himself draws me to be a stickler over this minor infraction. Having better sense than to initiate a confrontation at the beginning of class, I stalk my prey, waiting for the most opportune moment to strike.

I'm pleasingly surprised watching Willis complete all his work and participate pleasantly. When the time comes for Hard Work

Hump Day treats to be awarded, Willis poises the pencil in his ear and lounges back in his chair, folding his arms and expectantly smirking.

"Mr. Willis," I direct, "when all your supplies are turned in, you'll receive the candy you've earned for the day." I dismiss my better judgment as I choose to be bothered by his brash behavior.

"I already turned in my folder, Mr. Masters." His confidence conceals any chance of detecting the trap I've readied for him.

I set the spring, "Return the pencil as well, please."

"This is my pencil," he protests, indifferent.

"Youth are not allowed to carry personal pencils around the school," I explain. "And, that doesn't appear to be one of the golf pencils issued by the houses. It does look like," my finger peruses the master class list for effect, "one of the shiny new ones Mrs. McDonough is always putting out for her kids."

The fact that I've identified Willis's previous teacher ruffles him. He doesn't have to utter a sound to affirm I'm right.

"Well it's not yours." He tries to hide the desperation in his counter, but I can smell it.

"You're right," I partially concede. "If you turn it in, I'll be happy to get it back to Mrs. McDonough for you. If you don't, I'm afraid you can't earn your treat while breaking the rules." Framing my approach so all students present know there's no escape from my firm, yet fair, grasp, "I won't take your points because you worked really hard today. But, I'm afraid it's gonna have to be the pencil or the candy."

Willis leans over his desk incensed, waving the pencil at me. "This is bullshit!"

"Watch your mouth," I warn as I roll up my sleeve to coolly glance at a non-existent watch. "You have five seconds. And pick your words carefully because your points aren't guaranteed."

Defiantly, Willis leans back and crosses his arms, "Three, two . . ."

"Alright," he surrenders. "Here!" slamming the pencil on my desk. "Where's my candy?" he growls.

I savor the position of power. "Can you please make an appropriate request?"

"You're doin too much, Masters." His impotence seeps through, and he won't make a moral stand to leave empty-handed. "Please?" He dejectedly offers me an open palm without making eye contact.

"Thank you for making the right choice." I switch back to sincere. "The pencil issue in the school is a big deal with the principal. If you're going to pinch one," concluding my point with some practical advice, "don't be so cavalier about it."

Day 100

Routine is everything, and everything is routine. When stressed, our brain shuts off, and our body defaults to automated responses. The beginning of the day is a turbulent time; there's no telling who will show up to class, what mood will permeate the room, or if there'll be enough security to prevent pandemonium. The direction of the day is constantly in flux. Each decision made by a youth, YCO, counselor, teacher, and administrator creates butterfly ripples that impact everyone else.

I find comfort in my morning rituals. I park in the same row every day. I greet the gate guards, try to engage someone on the path to school with small talk, and hold the door for somebody else. Brightening someone's day usually has reciprocal influence.

Avoiding the front office is a covert affair. There is no telling when the boss will call you in to pile on something new. Scuttling straight upstairs, I store my lunch in the teacher's lounge refrigerator and use the facilities. Passing my class, I appreciate the current residents of haphazardly scattered tools and internet wires stacked to the ceiling. After going through the half-hour hullabaloo to enter the facility, tradesmen find it more efficient to leave the secured rooms they are working on in shambles to pick up where they left off the next day.

I retreat down the back stairs (which is technically forbidden) and offer a warm morning salute to a counselor who catches me. Entering class, I store my backpack in the most protected corner behind the desk and embrace a moment's pause.

Deep breath. Let's take on the day!

Jorge Masgeval, my one-man hype-train, is the first to greet me. "Where is everyone?" I inquire. It's five past nine and Jorge is my only attendee.

"I was with the chaplain," he stares off, down and past me. "My dad died."

We're alone in class, and there are no words I can offer to comfort this kid. "I'm sorry to hear that. Was he sick?"

"Nah. I think he died from smoking too much." Jorge is a phantom of his usually jovial, talkative self.

"I'm glad you got to talk to Chap." Uncomfortable does not begin to describe helplessly watching this kid after he was blindsided by the worst news he will probably ever receive. I insufficiently offer, "Tell me what I can do to help you today, okay?"

"Yeah." He slumps into a chair and rests his head on the desk, looking to one side with his hands hanging limp, inches above the floor. He's only 15 years old and burdened by his father's passing while stuck in jail. Little support is available: no mother and no family to lean on, to cry with.

Day 101

Finding reason to be excited despite my current classroom displacement, I'm giddy to give Lucas his Achievement of the Week Award. Lucas is one of the only genuine breakthroughs I've witnessed here. Breaking down to share his concern over his girlfriend and his wish to see his child born, I experienced his anguish. I yearn to assist him in his quest and hope my meager accolade can strengthen him on his way.

With all houses accounted for at the start of fourth period, I give a moment's pause. Lucas, who is usually the first one in attendance, has yet to appear. Inquiring of the audience, youth Aldridge reveals, "Lucas was in the middle of that brawl in the dietary. Six dudes were going at it. Security even brought out the mace." He laughs at the mayhem.

My other Achievement of the Week winner from the morning classes purportedly had his jaw broken by Antwon Bates. Evidently, my stellar scholar experienced a lapse of intelligence in an attempt to acquire the television remote from an obstinate Bates. Mr. Ellesberg won't be challenging anybody any time soon as he sips through a straw for the next four to six weeks.

Introducing my Award of the Week to new students leaves each young man covetous about earning a certificate (and the candy that goes with it). I've joked, in an attempt to quell them, it comes at a price. Roughly half my award winners have ended up in confinement the following week. I initially wrote off this trend as my ability to impact unsavory youth, but these two leave me with misgivings. Both are bright and articulate, outliers in our environment. I hitched to them in the hopes of a triumph in a tough place. The demise of both seems to verify that the Achievement of the Week could truly be cursed.

Moving forward with the day's lesson, I can't help but think: *Did I? Could I have caused these two to fall into some cosmic harm?* Fumbling through my prepared material, I second guess rewarding any more youth. *Could my requisites be stretching these kids beyond what they can handle? Am I rubber-banding them to failure?*

202

Day 103

Reinheriting Bates after a short reprieve, I find out his schedule has been altered, once again, after moseying into Ms. Green's class fully erect. Apparently this young man has the capacity to stand at attention without paying attention.

My attendance sheet also reveals that neither Ellesberg nor Lucas is assigned to my class any longer. After some snooping, I find that both Lucas and Ellesberg have been transferred to different facilities. Apparently, this is not Lucas's first rodeo. The "group" he referenced during our chat was anger management to help him with an explosive disorder, and his propensity for violence has led him to be upgraded to our maximum security facility up north. Ellesberg has been shipped straight to the infirmary of the special treatment facility. Upon awaking from surgery, Ellesberg exhibited non-stop panic and terror symptoms from the trauma. Clinical staff believe the only way to shake him from his current state is a change of scenery. The special treatment facility will service his needs while offering distance and protection from Bates.

Both Lucas's and Ellesberg's rewards linger, displayed on my board. I don't have the heart to take them down and am led to believe their stories can be used to teach a lesson to the rest. How to spin these stories to instruct other youth hasn't been revealed to me as of yet.

"Too much pussy in the world to be a homosexual." Aldridge brings me crashing back to the present.

"What in the world prompted that?" I have to ask.

"Lucas's bitchass was a gooch," Aldredge explains.

"A what?" I'm still disoriented, which is adding to the confusion of the moment.

"A gooch, you know, a gay dude," he clarifies.

"What does that have to with anything?" I'm perplexed to find a reason any of this is relevant.

"That's why Lucas kept getting into fights," Aldridge divulges. "Dudes be sayin he wears skinny jeans on the outs. Only bitches and skateboarders wear skinny jeans, and Lucas don't have no skateboard."

Leaving this thought hang too long, Aldridge fills the space, "Yo Masters, what do I gotta do to get a certificate?"

Happy to discuss a different topic, I answer, "Anyone can earn it if you go above and beyond the expectations."

"Alright, alright," he ponders. "I want one of those." Aldridge confidently nods as if his passing thought will make it a reality.

"You sure?" I'm still uneasy that the posted accolades read more like headstones. "Guys who end up on the board tend to run into a string of bad luck."

"Nah, those two were punks," Aldridge brushes it off. "Ain't nothing gonna happen to me."

At the close of the day, a chubby Hispanic young man requests an Atlas. Scanning the bookshelf, I'm surprised to find we're equipped with one. Garcia intensely immerses himself in the study of half-a-dozen pages. I'm admiring his fervor when he points out a path to a peer and comments, "Yeah man, we could smuggle AK's in from Alaska."

"What!?!" I'm thrown by the whiplash shift in perception.

"Sorry, Masters, but I gotta be a boss." Garcia puffs himself up to lay out his plans. "To be a boss, you gotta hold shit down. To control territory, you need money and power. Guns can get you both."

"Why Alaska?" I try to connect his line of thinking.

"The Mexican border is hot, man." I can't fault his accurate interpretation of current events. "AK's are Russian. They can get their product to Alaska, and then we can bring it home." Smiling, Garcia receives affirmation in the form of a fist bump from his peer.

"Shit gets real on the battlefield, motherfucker!" a pasty mouse in the corner explodes. Sims doesn't look up or even seem to acknowledge anything has been said; he just continues his daily ritual of copying words from the dictionary as if nothing's happened.

"What did you say, Sims?" I'm too stunned to be mad. His physical image doesn't fit the aggressive outburst and leaves me somewhat amused.

Sims quaveringly meets my gaze while pushing his glasses up his nose. I reassure him, "I'm not mad. I just can't believe what you said. Could you repeat it?"

"Shit gets real on the battlefield," much less convincing this go around, "motherfucker."

"Why in the world did you feel the need for that kind of eruption?" I feel stuck in an alternate dimension and can't wrap my head around what is motivating these kids.

"No reason." Sims shrugs and returns to his transcriptions. "It seemed apropos."

Day 104

"Good morning, everyone." Mike greats us joyfully at yet another unplanned morning meeting. There's a substantive sense of dread that accompanies these meetings. We're conditioned to suspect we're about to be force fed another pill without the courtesy of a spoonful of sugar. "I know we're a little behind schedule, but you'll be happy to know you'll be teaching upstairs this Friday." Mike pauses for applause. "After three-and-a-half weeks, all upstairs classrooms have an internet connection." He claps since no one else will. "Take the morning to resituate and clean your classrooms. Mrs. Stecker, Ms. Vasquez, Ms. Brown, Mrs. McDonough and Mr. Masters need to expedite the process because the Virtual Education trainer will be here at 9:30. Everyone else, check your boxes after lunch to get class lists for the next two days. And, for those who're ready to complain that they can't double up on kids, I know you've been doing it for over a week, so suck it up for the day-and-a-half." Mike slyly allowed our covert plan to combine kids and only teach half-a-day knowing he could strategically use it later. Kudos to him.

Transitioning homerooms is an occupational hazard for most teachers. In public school, summer break is traditionally used to clean and paint, and while rooms are vacated, administration can easily and effectively switch teachers' classrooms.

We, on the other hand, are moving back up to our classrooms with the looming possibility of having to move back down whenever the electrical is approved (no timeline). I've been commissioned to float among the three virtual classrooms in the mornings to ensure students with an IEP are being serviced (found out my new role corporately at this morning's meeting). Students will switch to a half-day schedule; two cottages attending in the morning and two in the afternoon will facilitate students ability to earn a pittance of the credit they should (the flimsy reason of "institutional growth" was given). Most assuredly the two unreplaced retired teachers and a transfer are to blame. A special education classroom shutting down to service online programming is icing on the cake.

Mike closes the meeting and comforts us with, "The only thing constant is change, people." My four new room assignments bring my institutional total to eight classrooms and six different preps in five months. The absurdity of pinballing around the school with no sense of control justifies my lack of investment in the continuity of the curriculum.

Perusing the disaster that once was my classroom, I don't delay in searching for a broom. Any skilled worker worth his weight will not clean up after himself because that is a waste of time and resources. Our tradesmen are no exception. It is evidently more cost effective to have a Master's level teacher paid to sweep floors. I don't fault the electricians; this was simply more poor planning on Mike's part. His inability to coordinate an inmate cleanup effort has led to a royal waste of our time.

Adding to the fun is the fact that my bookshelf had to be moved into a set of closets to accommodate the new wiring scheme. Intuiting the youth were involved in this effort because the shelf is actually restocked, I'm dismayed by whoever was in charge. To accommodate the shelf, someone removed the closet doors and stacked the contents precariously atop eight student desks. The bracketing that once held the doors remains either to allow reinstallation on a whim or because it is fused to the floor and walls. 'Twill remain a mystery.

Virtual Education Training entails a snooze-fest; we're to watch projected mock-up of the software we will be using. The presenter is not equipped with a handout because she finds it most effective for her students to follow along using a plug-and-play model. Kinesthetic teaching has proven the most effective model in learning new technologies.

We are ill-prepared as Ms. Brown uses the only computer station hook-up to enable our befuddled presenter with a projector. The teachers unite, using break time to set up five more stations in the hope that tomorrow we'll have internet access. Since each classroom is only equipped with one electrical receptacle along each wall, I entreat Mr. Park to locate enough extension cords with surge protectors from the woodshop to empower our training. His efforts are to no avail. Mr. Park rejoins us at the end of the day to reveal the already obvious fact that this institution is ill-equipped.

Day 106

Preferring to have a molar pulled over attending any more Virtual Education Training, I'm energized by the thought of another Friday teaching delinquents. Yesterday, Warden Pritz visited us with enough multiport power cords to set up all three computer classrooms. Though we had to couple the strands three to four deep, the building didn't brown out when all the computers whirred to life. In spite of Mike's email efforts, the internet connection to each desktop was not enabled until the final hour of the day, so at least three percent of our training was actually virtual. The VE trainer feebly attempted to rejuvenate us while presenting "You've been VETted" certificates which had to be inscribed by hand due to printer inaccessibility.

Entering another foreign classroom while not overly thrilled about the forced co-teaching arrangements, I find solace in the fact that I'm currently a glorified, overpaid tutor and leave the technicalities of the classroom to the teachers I visit.

Both periods, the youth are disoriented by the change. I'm sure the news of computer based classes was circulated, but the kids aren't given their schedules until they enter the school. *Who needs time to adapt to change?* Having your school and housing situation rearranged at a moment's notice is not new to these kids, but that doesn't make it normal.

We've been instructed to develop and cover expectations with our new wards and get them started on a virtual class. I suggested a warm-up or icebreaker activity to ease the kids' transition, but Mike kyboshed it on the premise that these boys need every minute available for credit recovery. To their credit, the youth adapt fairly well and most are able to progress through a partial lesson.

"Hands out." I've developed a ritual of announcing my Achievement of the Week winner. Instead of calling for applause, I attempt an athletically-inspired, unified, single clap with an over fifty percent success rate. "Jonas Aldridge is our winner this week for 'setting a goal and exhibiting diligent perseverance to accomplish it.'" Reading off the certificate I've drawn up, I hesitate to give it to

208

him because we haven't had class for the past two days. Resolving to monitor his participation this period, I'm compelled to award him because of the repentant tenacity he has exhibited over the past several days. I don't know how long he can keep it up, and I opt to reinforce it before it's too late.

Aldridge accepts the award and accompanying candy bar while warmly waving to his adoring public. "Thanks, Masters." His surprised yet appreciative grin is worth the price of admission.

Day 107

Trapped!

Unfortunate timing places me entering the front gate at the same time as Mike. "Happy Monday!" I grind my teeth while smiling. "How was your weekend?" Trading off my peers' strategy of keeping the enemy close, I don't know if I have the discipline to subdue violent ideations while security checks our bags.

"Oh, it was okay," he ponders. "I just painted my basement," he recalls, showing off his hands as merit badges of dried paint.

This man has single-handedly soured me to the teaching profession. I can handle deviant kids; I can hide from dismal coworkers; but I can't bear someone asininely turning the whole school upside down any time he's bumped his fucking head. "What was the color scheme?"

"Just white for now. I had to prime it a few times. The wife and I are still finalizing our thoughts. We think three taupe walls with a burgundy or lilac accent would be nice." I can't imagine the twit married to this buffoon.

The bathroom stationed just before the gatehouse exit is my salvation. I nod politely as I go in to relieve myself, unable to stomach another second of Mike's company.

Feeling a momentary twinge of guilt over my callous feelings toward Mike, I reaffirm my hostile stance on the remaining walk to school. I'm vindicated as a marathon of his slights and slanders plays through my mind. Besides, I remind myself, the Monday morning walkup is a bad time to get chummy with the boss. Mike is undoubtedly contemplating the laundry list of things to be accomplished this week. Keeping him company will almost assuredly earn me extra work before we get to the building.

The bathroom break-off was a masterful maneuver.

Even under the harshest of conditions (stranded, imprisoned, tortured) people can survive. The key to their survival is hope. When interviewed post trauma, most of those affected say there was a singular thought or person they held onto in order to persevere.

210

Waiting for me in the school foyer is despondency incarnate. "Oh, Jon, I meant to mention to you, I need you to sub for McDonough."

"Sub how? Where?" We haven't strung two days together under the new conditions, and Mike casually lobs another wrench into the already malfunctioning gears.

"I need you to play SPED floater all day. Mrs. McDonough has a doctor's appointment," *You couldn't have mentioned something sooner?* "and I want you to cover for her in the afternoon virtual classrooms.

"But," I meekly protest, "that needlessly puts my kids in the library. It's not like we're shutting down a classroom due to the lack of a teacher. She's just a floater and gone for one day," I appeal, extending my pointer finger in the futile attempt to illustrate a point.

"Mr. Masters," Mike condescends to over-assert his position. "We must keep up the validity of the study. In order to be valid," he sounds like he's reciting the letter of the manual, "there must be special education accommodations," without having a clue of its intentions.

Mike dismisses himself, confident his point has been made. Being too incensed to contest, I dazedly drift to my classroom. I silently vow to not do an ounce more work than is minimally necessary for the remainder of Mike's tenure.

"Oh, one more thing, Mr. Masters." Mike stalks me into Ms. Brown's class where I will serve as sub-floater for Mrs. McDonough. I've become desperate enough to think I need a restraining order to get away from this guy. "You're writing too many referrals."

This has got to be a joke. There is a hidden camera somewhere to capture the moment I crack. "What do you mean?"

"Well, I just got the data from Ms. Brown." He extends her a hand to applaud her effort. *Judas!* "It reveals that you wrote the second highest number of Time Out Tickets last month."

"TOTs are just one of the many interventions I employ." I've given up caring if I'm evaluated poorly. This incessant henpecking has got to end. "I've coordinated with Ms. Wells to process most of the youth I send to her. Mediating with the youth while clarifying

211

my expectations has led to a change in student behavior." Not being able to hide my exasperation, I beg that he relent, just one time.

He's unflappable. "I appreciate all your efforts. I'd like to see you write less referrals."

My better senses tell me to leave this be, but I can't live in fear of his next kneejerk reaction that'll spread shit all over my sandbox. "I would like to write less, believe me. It's difficult being the new teacher and having to establish my style and authority with a population that tests every limit. This has been compounded by the fact that I've taught in over half-a-dozen different classrooms already. Each time is like a new beginning. And, it takes time, routine, and discipline to get the kids on board." Breathlessly finishing my plea, I hope for any shred of decency Mike might have in reserve to appear in this moment.

"Well, I need you to do something different." Mike leaves this hang, daring me to object as the candid camera producer zooms in on my temple vain.

Youth Jorge Masgeval disrupts my eruption, entering the classroom between us. "I thought you were paroled?" I inquire surprisedly. Mike uses the diversion to waddle away. He stared me down, and I didn't respond. In his mind, he's won.

"Yeah, man," Jorge divulges. "My mom can't get a ride out here, Homes."

"So, when will you be able to get out?" It's a disheartening distraction to see paroled kids stuck here a moment in excess of his sentence.

"I think they'll ship me to the city facility Friday. My mom said she'd take three buses to meet me there." Though disheartened by the extension of his sentence, he beams at the display of motherly love.

Day 109

Kids avoiding class is an epidemic! At least a dozen roam the halls in packs for fifteen minutes while a single security guard ineffectively attempts to herd the horde to class. The students perceive they've got us outnumbered, and in some bizarre attempt at equity, if we can't capture them all, we consequence none.

The first time Aldridge whirs by, he pretends not to hear me. The second time, I get a response. Aldridge maintains a consistent gate while casually raising one arm to flip me the bird before returning it to his side.

I'm torn on how to handle this situation. Aldridge has done more than enough to merit a Time Out Ticket, but Mike is closely tracking my TOTs. It appears the guards have their hands full, and I could just as well close my door and pretend nothing happened. I never saw him.

The guilt gnaws at me as class gets underway. That type of defiance shouldn't go unchecked, and being my reigning Achievement of the Week recipient, I consciously hold him to a higher standard because I've seen that he's capable. If something has disturbed him enough to deviate this far from baseline, I resolve a therapeutic intervention is in order to inhibit further harm.

Finishing the TOT and giving it to security, I attach a sticky note for Ms. Wells to bring Aldridge back to process. If we can sort things out, I'll tear up the referral and consider our intervention sufficient. This should build rapport with all present to witness my acts of mercy.

Assuming Ms. Wells has received my note, I greet her amicably at the door. "Where's Aldridge?" I'm puzzled by the absence of the youth.

"I thought he was yours," she explains. "He's been running amuck since the start of transition. I wanted his assigned teacher to write him up."

"I did. You mean you didn't get it?"

"Nope." Wells purses her lips pensively while shaking her head.

"I wrote a TOT and attached a note that I wanted to process with him." I get her up to speed. "Mike's on my ass about writing too many kids up, so I wanted to see if we could cut Aldridge a break after talking it through and tear up the TOT since he's had a lot of success in my class lately."

"Well I don't think he's in the mood. He has cursed out or threatened half-a-dozen staff who've tried to intervene," Wells explicates. "He's already been sent to Truman to cool off. Paperwork has to follow shortly, or they'll cut him loose."

"Is there any way you can sign it?" I plead. "I'm willing to write it up, but I'm working to keep my paperwork numbers low."

Wells places a reassuring hand on my shoulder. "Disciplinary tickets don't get reported the same way TOTs do. Mike doesn't have to know you wrote this one." Wells starts to fade down the hall. There appear to be more fires to extinguish. Turning back, "Get the paperwork to me, and I'll see to it that it goes straight to Truman without crossing Mike's desk. Include all the time Aldridge has been out of class and the number of staff he cursed out so the charges stick." Wells disappears around the corner, leaving me with a room full of students and a small pile of paperwork.

The lesson gets away from me as the boys are too squirrely to let me finish the ticket. Unable to tell whether or not it's a strategy to help their comrade-in-arms avoid trouble, I change gears to focus on teaching the youth. Fully aware that the security structure heavily favors expediently finishing reports over any and everything else, I can't bring myself to put more effort into punishing one over educating the mass. Aldridge makes no reappearance, and I'm able to piecemeal the ticket together over the closing period.

Mrs. McDonough begrudgingly accepts my sole remaining youth during dismissal to allow me to deliver Aldridge's ticket to Juvenile Supervisor Martin, the lead officer for the day. "You know this is a minor charge. His counselor isn't going to do anything with it," Martin deprecates after a summary glance.

"I was instructed to write it because he was sent to confinement." I hold my hands up surrendering as messenger. "Do with it what you will." Wiping my palms, "It's out of my hands."

My periphery catches Youth Higgins lounging in a holding pen where youth wait for a transport to deliver them to a requesting staff

214

(counselor, therapist, job). "Where were you today?" I inquire, socially.

Higgins smirks out the left side of his mouth. "Didn't feel like coming to class."

"Were you part of the hallway mob earlier?" I'm more interested than accusatory.

"Yep. They piled us in a van to Truman but ran out of rooms, so I've been hanging here all day." Higgins rises, which startles me. I follow his gaze to JS Martin, waving him to the exit. "Peace out, Masters. I gotta work."

Befuddled by the winding chain of events, my curiosity leads me to ask, "Mr. Martin, that kid avoided class all afternoon, and now he gets to go to work?"

"Hey man, I just got here." Martin's on the defensive now. "If I get some paperwork on him, I'll see what I can do. Otherwise, he reports to dietary."

"Forget it." I've chased the wind enough for one day.

Day 110

My dress has become considerably more casual. Adopting a wardrobe of hoodies, jeans, and gym shoes has enhanced my relations with the full population of youth. Nearly a dozen times a week, a youth, familiar or not, stops me to ask about my apparel. Knowing these boys spend exorbitant amounts on their flash and flair, I capitalize on the opportunity to educate the young men about bargain hunting and the merits of thrifty shopping. They are astounded entire ensemble costs less than a pair of their shoes or jeans. When I explain the merits to living simply to pay down debts and build savings, they must wrestle with the age old question of living for the moment or living for the long-haul.

Moseying into the SBS meeting this morning, I'm unclear where I stand with the point system discussion. Though I've followed through on Ms. Paulsen's suggestions, Mike's made no further mention of any implementation plans. Equipped with a couple of samples, I've prepared an itinerary that makes mention of continuing the conversation.

"Jon, glad I caught you." Mike waddle-jogs to catch me before I enter the library. I notice four rows set up with at least 30 people lounging around. "I need you to present the idea that you and Mindy came up with regarding the points."

Immediately regretting my fashion decisions, "How many people are we talking here?"

"I'd say 50 to be safe." Mike brushes past me in pursuit of the Warden and Chief of Security.

Completely unprepared to train this throng on an unapproved prototype, I fake it with panache. First, I review the institutional intention to further SBS's positive principals. Then, I illustrate our current model's inadequacies. The big finish expounds over the evolution of the point card and the necessity for it to be pliable. Naturally segueing, I open up to the room for suggestions. Not a hand in the bunch goes up.

Mike quickly relieves me with, "Thank you Mr. Masters," and introduces Ms. Brown to present the historical context of SBS in the institution. The stone-faced stoicism of the group makes them difficult to gauge. It's also quite unnerving. Championing a system that requires cooperative investment, I haven't a clue where I stand with the people.

The group is dismissed to accept the entering youth to the school, but the Warden catches my arm. "Mr. Masters, won't you join us in Mr. Hicks's office to discuss implementation plans for your point card?"

Enthusiastically responding, "Absolutely!" I peer at Mike for permission. "What should I do with my kids?"

"Instruct security to divert them to the library. You can pick them up when we finish." Mike appreciates his reinsertion onto the high seat of this house.

Falling in line with the parade, I'm giddy over the feather in my cap, and my mind races, teasing out the possibilities. The Warden gets the ball rolling. "In your mind, what's it gonna take to change the institution over to your sheet?"

Finding it difficult to withhold from beaming in the spotlight, I quickly switch to all business. "We need more buy-in for SBS. To ensure everyone is on board, we should first inform and collaborate with the professional staff to work out the programmatic kinks of a new point structure so that all departments and youth are serviced by the switch. Then, we'll need to train security. Once that is done, pick a Monday. We should be able to seamlessly transition because our levels and programming are already in place and will stay the same."

"Very good." The Warden moves to the edge of his seat. "Mr. Hicks, can you coordinate with the necessary department heads to get everyone on board? Thank you for your hard work, Mr. Masters." The Warden's assurance is conveyed through captivating eye contact as he closes the meeting with a firm handshake.

My boys buck like broncos when I wrangle them out of the library, but even their bemoaning can't dampen my excitement.

"I'm ready to pop off in this bitch!" Aldridge skips through the door making a lap around the classroom.

"You know the deal. Just sit quietly, and I'll let you be." I know this line is a blow-off, but at least one student per day has a life-or-death meltdown. I find it's best to minimize empathy in these cases for peace of classroom.

Once the class is steadily working, I pull a chair in front of Aldridge's desk. His pain looks legitimate, and I feel a twinge of guilt for blowing him off. "What's bothering you?"

"I got bad news, and Tuck's bitch-ass wrote me up. Fuck this place."

Trying to focus his angst to address the root, I probe, "What was the bad news?"

"My sister died." This kid can't buy a break. I'm astounded he was able to pull it together as well as he did after his mom passed suddenly two months ago. (The Achievement of the Week curse is real.) That news led him to punch out a pane glass window in his counselor's office, which led to 11 stitches. His right hand was bandaged to the elbow at her funeral. I was floored to find that he almost wasn't permitted to go due to his mental state. Chalk one up for decency.

"Did you just find out?" I continue to encourage him to share his burden.

"Yeah. My dad's wife called to tell me over the weekend. Well, she was my dad's wife, but he died." How is this kid standing, much less in school?

My heart breaks for this poor soul. I want to move mountains to ease this kid's sorrow. Sadly, the institutional policy is, "We don't have the staff to sit one-on-one for an extended period of time." Blanket statements are of no use for the truly broken.

Attempting to lighten his burden, I ask, "See that quote on the board?" Aldridge continues his desk stare. "Find joy in your suffering because suffering builds perseverance, perseverance builds character, and character gives way to hope. I think that is Romans 5:3-4." Although we're given latitude with the separation of church thing because these kids are so far gone, I don't push for writing down the actual verse. It's best to leave it as ambiguous wisdom while on display in my class. Reciting the book and line always makes me feel a phony kind of self-righteous, though I like to believe I'm not. "You have to just keep trying to put one foot in front of the other." I emphasize one last ideal to convince us both to believe it. "It will get better in time."

I leave him to saturate with this thought. Though time doesn't heal everything, his pain will callous over, and he'll find a way to live with the scar tissue regardless of the extent of its visibility.

Aldridge leaves his seat to pace aggressively wall-to-wall in the back of the classroom. Usually, I don't allow this because movement makes seated students squirm. There are only three other kids present, and if roving keeps him in his skin, God Bless him.

<u>Day 111</u>

High Five Fridays have a tendency to get slap happy. As we wait for the kiddies to progress to our rooms, Casey and I engage in a philosophical conversation down the hallway:
"This place cracks me up sometimes," I begin.
Casey kindly corrects, "You mean to say, 'you're a crack up because of this place.'"
"Ha!" I retort, happy for the chance to let off some steam. "Yeah, dealing with the mediocrity for this long is getting to me."
"Are you kidding?" Casey quips. "Mediocrity is a step up from us. I would strive for and embrace mediocrity. In fact, if Mike was good for nothing, that would be an improvement." Casey hoots at his own dig, and I'm a little worried our boss could be lurking and discover us. I'm not as bold as the rest yet, but I'm finding confidence in the fact that my probation will be ending soon, and in the meantime, they can't fire the point-card guy. I mean, the warden knows my name.
Adding to Casey's assessment, "We're fully capable of being mediocre. Mediocrity could happen if our boss took a more hands-off approach. The problem lies in the fact that we take the mediocre," I pretend to knead dough and progress to a thrashing frenzy, dropping it to the floor, "and fuck it up."
"Abysmal?" Casey suggests.
"Nah, that's too negative." I defend my new home. "The people here try. They really do. But, our attempts just make it worse. The attention suffocates it. We need to pinpoint a positive word a rung lower than mediocre."
"Failing?"
"Still negative," I protest. "What sounds nice but ranks between mediocre and abysmal?"
(Contemplative silence)
Casey lights up. "Incompetent!"
I put a bow on it, "Utterly Incompetent. U I!"
"It shows we try." Casey defines our new status professorially. "We just can't help how bad we make things. U I is perfect. We can even make gang-sign hand-signals to better capture the moments as

they happen without Mike being the wiser." He struggles at first but settles for cupping his full hand into a 'U' then flicking me off.

"When we're in public we'll have to settle for a pointer," I illustrate.

"Even better." Casey makes the 'U' followed by a thumbs up with a cheesy smile.

"Perfect!"

Day 113

Yet another "No school" Tuesday. This job is tasking physically, mentally, emotionally, and spiritually. Just when I think I've reached the end of my tether, manna is dropped in the form of a posted paper announcing a respite. I'm tempted to skip to my room.

Because of the infusion of extra time, I feel compelled to socially celebrate. We can corporately bask in the good vibes until 9:00 when Mike sweeps the upstairs hallway to ensure teachers are working diligently. My first source of comradery is Casey, but before I can reach him to jubilate, I notice Casey appears to have been crying. I offer a cautious, "Good morning," and perceive puffy red eyes before Casey can conceal them.

Leaving him to weep, I feel guilty but would be more comfortable subduing a junky laced-out on PCP than offering someone my shoulder to cry on. I sequester myself to avoid a corporate cry-fest that could progress into any open room.

I'm not left long to ponder before Mike interrupts on the intercom. *"Teachers, please report the school office. Thank you. CLICK."*

Oblivious to any possible cosmic connectedness, I procure a seat and wait for Mike to resurface from his closed office. The rest of the teachers file in with a chorus of chuckles, cheery over school cancelation. Mike emerges from his office wearing fresh tears of his own. "I was informed, late last night, that Mrs. Stecker passed away suddenly." As if on cue, Casey joins us, somberly sniffling. Mike must have been compassionate enough to let Casey know his friend had passed before telling the group. "There aren't a lot of details. Preliminary results indicate a blood clot caused an aneurysm in the brain, which led to a stroke. The doctors said there was little chance of reviving her."

Mike allows a moment of silence for the immensity and gravity to settle upon the staff. "We won't be having school today to allow for a period of mourning. I'm meeting shortly with Warden Pritz and the clinical teams to make a plan to break the news to the youth. Mrs. Stecker was part of our family, and we've suffered a great loss today. My door is open. Please, offer comfort and support to one another today."

Too stunned to move, I remain catatonic, trying to compartmentalize the devastation. I've only been here a short time and didn't know Mrs. Stecker well. Every interaction we had was clipped by her brashness. *How am I supposed to feel about the death of a woman I didn't know and, frankly, didn't care for?* Deciding the appropriate amount of time has passed, I solemnly rise and present a mindfully distraught persona for the benefit of those more effected by this tragedy.

"Jon," Mike has his coat in hand and waves me to follow. "Warden Pritz would like you to sit in on our meeting."

Pritz is a snappy dresser with precision hair. Being younger middle-aged, he initially appeared to be a social climber. Pritz reversed my aspersions last month by attending the latter half of the Bible study in the school and praying over his personnel. Upon his exit, staff members touted his compassionate leadership.

"I want to begin by saying Mr. Hicks, Mr. Masters, and all those who knew Patricia Stecker well, my heart breaks for your loss. Boys Home faces a tough road ahead, mourning the loss of a family member. I have gathered you all here to collaborate a way to deliver the news to the kids in the most sensitive, supportive fashion. Also, on behalf the mental health department, all counselors and therapists are at the full disposal of the school for the remainder of this week and the next for any teachers that need to grieve. Before we continue, I'd like to pause for a moment of silence over the departed."

Though Pritz is a vibrantly Christian man, he intuits that, even in such an overwhelming moment, praying corporately in the workplace is too tumultuous. "Thank you. I'd like to take the opportunity to use housing conferences to share the news and counsel our kids. Each counselor should bring at least two therapists with them to offer grief services to the youth. If the youth take the news particularly hard, please focus on processing the grief over completing all the conferences. We can complete them down the road if need be." Pritz scans the room to receive approving nods. "Mr. Hicks, I'd like to gather the teachers again with the clinical supervisors present to offer our condolences and make them aware of the available support network."

"Agreed," Mike's down to business.

"Mr. Masters," My names is a shock to my awareness. "I would like to offer to pray over the teaching staff at the end of the meeting. Would you be willing to close the prayer?"

Death takes a while to hit me. The announcement usually doesn't floor me. Even the body in the box can't bring me to tears. Only a moment they should be with us makes me feel and recognize their absence. I tentatively reply, "Of course," because that's what people do in these circumstances, offer comfort.

Day 114

Emptiness accompanies me on the walk from my car to the gate as I question why some sort of emotion isn't welling up inside me. Meeting Ms. Grimly, I offer a muted pleasantry and accompany her on the long walk to the school. "How'd your kids take the news yesterday?" I casually question.

"Take what news?" she's answers obliviously. "I wasn't here yesterday. I just got back from vacation."

"So, no one told you?" Holding my hand over my mouth, I want to display the appropriate sentiment. "Mrs. Stecker passed away Monday."

"Oh my gosh! I'm so sorry." She grabs my arm for support. "What happened?"

"They're not certain but believe she had a stroke."

"Poor thing. I'll be praying for her family." Ms. Grimly, a church lady, is a beacon of comfort. "How are you taking it?"

"Honestly, I didn't know her well." The lump in my gut begins to lessen. "We never really hit it off, and I don't know how to act around the teachers who knew her well." There is a surprising catharsis in revealing the cloudy truth.

"Well Mr. Masters, I think sometimes a quiet presence is all we're called to be. Nothing we say is going to lessen the pain. People die, and no one has found a good way to take away the sting. Offer comfort where you can. It'll take time for this tragedy to pass."

"Thank you Ms. Grimly." We spend the remaining walk silently prepping to attend to the hurting.

Gliding through the motions of the morning, I've made it to my classroom unsure of the plans going forward. During all the meetings, we never addressed how to reopen the school and receive the youth. Mike interrupts my contemplative questions with unfortunate answers. "Mr. Masters, I need you to teach Patricia's classes this morning." He takes a laboured breath, having delivered his message after the journey from his lower level office.

My confused, wordless reply encourages Mike's clarification. "You'll be in her class in the morning, and Mrs. McDonough will teach the afternoons."

I'm stupefied. "Today?"

"Yes," Mike checks his watch. "I want you down there by 8:30 to receive the kids. Ms. Brown will help you with the ins and outs of running a Virtual classroom. You can email her with questions."

"You can't be serious." My composure is lost. "We just found out yesterday she died. Stecker taught in there on Monday, and today, you want me to lead her class? Can't we have a week?" I plead. "I'll take her kids into my classroom. Please; it's just too soon."

"I understand your hurting, Mr. Masters, but we have a job to do." Mike leaves me with the most sincerity and compassion he can muster.

"Masters, man! You so lame. I saw you sittin between those two bitches lookin. . ." Bates sits with a stiff posture, hands and legs together, bug-eyed, and statuesque to impersonate me. "Man! I woulda been hollerin at those hoes."

At first, his flagrantly flippant comments fly over my head. Realizing he's referencing the fact that I was sitting between two mental health interns while his counselor delivered the news that his teacher had died, I'm at a loss of where to start. Should I begin with the way he addresses women, the fact that I'm married, the fact that it is borderline harassment to hit on a colleague, or the fact that I'm currently sitting in a dead woman's chair?!?

Too much time passes as I ponder a response. "Man! You ain't got no game. You gay or something?"

In no mood to verbally spar, I keep it sparse, "Mr. Bates, do your work," *before I lose it.*

"Yo! Those bitches were fine. Uh! I woulda . . ." He demonstrates an exaggerated humping motion, bringing his hands from shoulders to crotch as he thrusts out of his seat several times while grunting. "Masters, you gotta hit that."

"Mr. Bates, number one, it is inappropriate to speak to staff this way about sex. Number two . . ."

"Man, you are a homo. Wasted yo chance."

226

"Number two, Mr. Bates, one of your teachers just died. Even if you don't have strong feelings about the subject, please be respectful of those who are feeling the loss."

"You just bein a straight up bitch, Masters."

I've no patience left for this kid. "Bates, stop talking. Do your work, or leave!"

"I got you, I got you." This may be the first time he's ever relented. I don't know if it might be a burgeoning ounce of compassion or my teaching interactions taking effect. "I'm just sayin."

"Stop 'sayin.' Start workin." Turning to my computer screen for refuge, I've chosen to avoid disciplinary interactions because this isn't . . . wasn't my class. The transitionary realization brings tears to my eyes.

"Where's Steck?" Thompson wanders in late.

Bates illuminates him. "She's dead, dude."

"Nah, really?" Thompson looks to me for answers.

My eyes well as I have no choice but to blindside this kid. "She passed away on Monday."

"For reals?" Thompson takes a step back, bringing both hands up to cup the top of his head.

"Who's your counselor?" I have to know where the breakdown occurred.

"Ms. Grimly, why?"

Already knowing the answer, "Didn't anyone visit Washington yesterday during conferences to tell you guys?"

"We didn't have conferences, Masters. Ms. Grimly's been out." Thompson still hasn't changed locations, frozen from registering the bombshell.

"So, nobody told you?"

"First I heard was now." Looking down to compose himself, he meets my gaze, "Why are we having school?"

"You're guess is as good as mine." I empathize with the young man so we can collectively get beyond the pain.

Accusatorily, "Why are you teaching in Steck's class?" Thompson becomes protective his fallen teacher's territory.

"Mr. Hicks asked me to."

"You could've said no." He's hurt by the perception that Mrs. Stecker is not missed enough to have an enshrined room.

227

Opening a window into my world, I reveal, "I wasn't really given a choice."

With the wisdom of the ages, Thompson closes our conversation, "That's fucked up, man," and finds a computer to begin his classwork.

Day 115

It's astonishing how blasé these boys are over continuing their education in a dead teacher's classroom. Only two days out, and their presented appearance doesn't acknowledge anything has transpired.

Mulling over the ineffectualness of the youth with Casey at lunch, he poses the question, "What did you expect?"

Contemplating the question, "I honestly thought more of them would be hurting or at least creeped out by having to stay in that classroom." This type of forthright conversation helps us both heal.

"At 41, she was an old lady to them." Casey shares a glimpse into the juvenile perspective. "Most of these kids don't believe they'll make it to 25. Stecker had a husband and kids. She lived a good long life in their minds."

Even though I know he's right, I can't fathom accepting that darkness could be instantaneously permanent at that age. I thought I was invincible through my mid-twenties. I didn't think I could ever die, and these kids feel it's a certainty. I guess both philosophies are reckless.

"You going straight to the wake today?" I further the small talk.

"Yeah." He looks down. "That's why I wore the slacks."

"You taking the whole day tomorrow or coming back after the wake?"

"Whole day. The teachers are meeting at *The Tavern* afterward," he shares. "You should come. We can get drunk and fondly remember our sister-in-arms. My wife offered to pick us up if we reminisce too long."

"Thanks," I chuckle. "I may take you up on that."

Two cars destined for collision. The boys are allowed to bring in a magazine to read during break times in the computer classes. I witness a snatch. "Mr. Dante, you need to ask permission before you take someone's things."

Tires screech. "Give me my mother fuckin magazine!" I've inadvertently alerted youth Dodge to the crime.

Wheels turn. "Mr. Dodge, please have a seat." I implore him to let me handle the situation.

Impact is inevitable. "You better get the fuck back!" Dante responds to the aggression.

Dodge grabs the magazine. CRASH!!! Dante stands and pulls the magazine back. Dodge grabs his shirt. The magazine is forgotten as each youth attempts to bear hug and lift the other off the ground.

After allowing a couple minutes of what can only be described as ineffective Greco-Roman wrestling (they've held firmly to each other's torso trying to throw their opponent to the ground), security separates them. No punches are thrown.

Mike storms into the room five minutes later as I'm processing the papers. "What happened?"

I can't tell if he's here to check up on my condition or if he's more worried about the equipment. Most likely the equipment. "Possibly the silliest fight I've ever seen." The peanut gallery falls into hysterics. The class loves it. Even I'm led to grin over some much needed levity.

Day 116

It feels foreign to don a button-down and tie. Dress shirts restrict movement, and a tie can be a choking hazard. For defensive purposes, both have been dismissed from my daily attire.

Arriving late for the proceedings, I settle into a back pew stage left. Scanning the room, I locate my conglomerate and receive some welcoming nods.

The priest leads the procession with Widower Stecker on his heels. In his arms, a wispy pre-school aged girl in a shimmery silver dress finds comfort on her father's shoulder. The middle son, six, holds dad's right hand while the oldest, nine, stoically flanks his sister.

For the entire drive to *The Tavern*, I'm dedicated to shaking the image of that little girl. At such a formative age, love is simply expressed and felt through a warm lap and available arms. That poor child's pool of love has been shrunk by half.

The crew arrives, and we drown our collective pain in a pint. Lashonda and Mike's delayed arrival is accompanied by the explanation that they went to the gravesite. The once healing revelry instantly deflates around these two. As if a recording device has been placed in the middle of the seating, all parties clam up to finish their drinks and expediently move on with their lives, not wanting to self-incriminate.

Annie extends support as she offers to cancel a long-standing girls' night to comfort me. Aware that I'd prefer to be alone, she accepts my false show of strength and leaves me in peace.

The bottles stack up as the night progresses, and just before the sun sets, I decide I need a walk. Lighting a cigar and sipping beer from a disguising water bottle, I embrace the darkness as it washes over me:

Drinking is not a means of escape.
I don't bask in drunkenness to get away from the shit I've seen, the abuse I've endured.
It's punishment.
Punishment for the things I didn't do.

Punishment for the things I KNOW I should have done, could have done.

I smoke because I'm too much of a coward to kill myself.
Each breath, meant to be my last.
But, it doesn't end.

Day 119

Normal has reemerged. The travesties of a week ago, the shameful mishandling of a departed colleague, have been covered by fear of repercussion and need for employment. Deep down, the teachers didn't really expect anything different. New tragedy uncovers a deep seeded hope for salvation, if only fleeting. Idealism is quickly abandoned out of necessity.

Mike's abrupt, down-to-business greeting blindsides me again this morning. There will be a conference in my honor, at which I shall bestow the masses with the design, execution, and implementation of the new point card. Having momentarily lost the drive to climb the ladder of advancement, I'm unprepared to tactfully tackle my boss. "Mike, you can't spring huge things like this on me out of the blue. If this new point system is going to work, I need time to ready a presentation."

"Well, you have until ten." His chipper go-get-'em attitude disguises the fact that there is no other choice; comply or be reprimanded. "Your students will go to the library this morning, and you can use your new computer to get things ready." I'm repulsed by the revelation that Mike enthusiastically believes a deceased woman's classroom is a promotion for my hard work. "I'll meet you here at five to ten, and we can walk over together." Mike wants a firm reign of his show horse to bask in the proximity accolades.

Knowing full well that this may be the last time this idea is mine, I go to work breaking it down to its simplest form. Beyond this meeting, the point card will need to be disseminated to 350 employees. I toil knowing, at the heart, I truly want to make a positive impact on these kids even if that means someone else runs with it.

At ten, I'm fidgety and debate leaving Mike. I will myself to find patience to wait longer when I realize he is my only source of knowledge that this meeting is happening and he will make me suffer if I show him to be tardy.

We enter the administrative conference room and greet Warden Pritz at ten past. The room is half full, and more are pouring in. I

233

realize I've grossly underestimated my audience and excuse myself to make more copies. The snail's pace of the antiquated copy machine only accentuates the fact that I'm late and underprepared. I reenter to find a full house with some standers in the back and try not to panic over the fact that I'm about to address a crowd of veteran professionals with the idea that I've discovered a better way of doing things in less than six months on the job.

After an awkward introduction from Mike, he and Warden Pritz retreat from the line of fire leaving all eyes on me. Starting with my background and all the initials I've been affiliated with to conceal my inexperience, I deliver my pitch. To my surprise, the audience is eerily receptive. Emboldened, I make a strong finish, appealing to collaboratively continue to develop and evolve positive programming that improves our care of these youth. With that said, I welcome questions and comments to clarify and unify the room.

A solitary question from the group comes by way of a nurse. "When will this take effect?"

I look to Warden Pritz for an answer, and he seems pleased to announce, "Next week security will be trained, and the following Monday, this will go live."

"That seems awfully quick," Counselor Smithe objects.

Supportively, I defend my proposal. "I know change can be difficult. Strategic Behavior Systems is just a tool to add to our belts that helps the youth. This point card is another tool. Our levels and rewards are already strongly established, so this shouldn't make too many waves," I reassure.

Warden Pritz dismisses everyone with a "thank you," and I find strength in the smiles, nods, and even a couple of handshakes I receive in affirmation. This is going to happen. The point card is only a small tweak in the much needed overhaul of our institutional culture, but it starts a mindset shift which is critical. This is going to work.

Warden Pritz promises to email a training schedule detailing when I will appear at the pre-shift roll call meetings next week. Like a pubescent girl, I can't wait to see if he's called. Instead of a letter from the warden, I receive an email from Mike with instructions to meet with the counselors this afternoon at three. Mistakenly, Mike includes the entire chain of emails. The previous one is a request from Ms. Robins, the clinical supervisor, for the meeting, and that was spurred on by Mrs. Veal, a counselor who was present at today's training.

Mrs. Veal's irritation is audible as I read, *"This is unacceptable. We're having a completely new system dumped in our laps without having any say. Can you call a meeting to discuss this new system before it's too late?"*

Back to the adversarial roll, I puzzle over why none of the counselors spoke up during the earlier sessions.

Equipped with the same packets I previously disseminated, I make the lonely walk across the street to the clinic. I stop by Mike's office to accompany him again, but he gives me a thumbs up vote of confidence with the phone cradled between shoulder and cheek. "You can handle this."

Finding shelter in the familiar space of Ms. Grimly's office, I inquire, "What's all this about?"

"You have a very good idea, Mr. Masters," she encourages. "Some counselors have their feathers in a ruffle. Only Mr. Smithe and Mrs. Veal will be there anyway. Answer their questions, and we'll all move on our merry way." She smiles, reassuringly adding, "You'll be fine."

Ms. Robins retrieves and escorts me to a conference room where Mr. Smithe and Mrs. Veal are already seated, seething. Ms. Robins opens, "Mr. Masters, my counselors have asked me to call a meeting to clarify this new point card because its implementation will be a big part of their jobs."

"I'm happy to help," I tell Ms. Robins, trying to avoid the glare.

"Go ahead." Ms. Robins opens the floor with an upturned hand.

Mr. Smithe hems and haws trying to find professional words to express his frustration. "Mr. Masters, how long have you worked here at Boys Home?"

"Almost six months," I reply coolly. This information has nothing to do with the matter at hand, and I know he's heading towards undermining my credibility due to lack of experience, but I answer it anyway to not appear combative.

"And what makes you think you have enough experience with these youth to critique or change a long established system?" he levels.

235

"I'll admit, I don't have a ton of experience here." I attempt to take away some ammo. "But, I do have seven years teaching in three different behavior schools and running behavior management programming." I leave the answer curt to force the line of questioning back on the aggressors.

"Are you aware that a new point sheet was proposed five years ago?" Smithe slides another format over to me.

As I peruse the newly introduced evidence, I reveal, "I was not aware."

"Because you weren't here," Smithe jabs and quickly continues to avoid scrutiny from Ms. Robins. "This document was introduced by Mr. Shoemaker and myself to the previous Warden. It was shelved. I believe it is as viable as yours. Why wasn't it introduced as well, and why has yours been pushed through?"

"This is the first I've ever seen this," I admit, "and I like how it defines expectations to be scored." Smithe's version is essentially a check list of 'yes' and 'no' next to skills that should be present throughout the day. "It does seem a bit rigid though," I continue. "These are the expectations, no doubt, but we want to leave room for the kids to go beyond, to grow and improve. Also, it seems very black and white. There is no room for partial credit, which I think will hurt rapport building for the staff."

"These kids need discipline!" Mr. Smithe interjects. "As a former security officer, I know how to run a house and get these kids to march in line." Smithe accentuates his point with a bout of overly aggressive, rapid pointing to his proposal.

"Easy Mr. Smithe," Ms. Robins coaches. "Mr. Masters is here to help, not get heckled."

"I agree with you about the discipline." I attempt to find common ground. "But, a rigid system leaves very little room to build high level traits. I do want to make the expectations clear and give security a tool to teach and enforce them. I wish you were at the SBS meetings because you have some very valid points based on a great deal of experience."

That hits home and takes the wind out of his sails. The counseling staff has always been invited to SBS meetings but uniformly refuses, and Ms. Robins is forced to represent the department alone.

"Why is the school given so many points?" Mrs. Veal accuses, taking up the torch.

"The committee agreed that school needs to be a high priority," I deflect, sharing the decision making process with colleagues. "Boys Home's Mission Statement decrees that 'education reduces recidivism.' Also, the school is the only place the housing populations intermingle. It was decided that the school needed some clout to reinforce the higher functioning skills to be successful in that environment."

A lengthy pause allows my opponents to stew, but neither come up with any more objections. "Thank you for your time, Mr. Masters." Ms. Robins dismisses me while shuffling her papers.

"Any time." I twist the knife as I turn to exit. "If you have any questions, feel free to email me."

Day 121

The energy is high in the school today because of graduation. The teachers aren't necessarily thrilled over the academic milestone; it just means we have a Friday afternoon with no school.

Casey takes it seriously, dressed in a suit and tie. He has accepted the roll of Master of Ceremonies because three of the four graduates are his GED kids. The majority of our boys are unable to achieve the credits necessary for graduation due to the constant transitioning between schools. Most of them have been kicked from regular to alternative schools, then arrested and brought to county jail schools, only to be transferred to our state facility after sentencing. Upon release, they continue the cycle. Those entering our school with any sort of promise are immediately funneled into the GED track. Any form of diploma statistically increases the chances of these kids succeeding.

Mr. Santarini has rejoined the fold as our guest speaker for the graduates. Neither students nor staff are overjoyed to see him, but those he approaches greet him warmly. Santa focuses his speech around his many years of teaching and the students he's impacted. He tries to relate growing up in an Italian neighborhood in the 1950s to the kids' current plight but comes off as out-of-touch and slightly racist.

Casey concludes the ceremony by introducing the valedictorian. "When this young man came to me, he was angry and frustrated by the process and amount of work. More than once, we had to sit down with Mr. Hicks, our principal, to convince young Mr. Sanchez to stick with it. I even remember him saying, 'if I don't pass the qualifier, I quit.' Well, you've made it! Would you like to say a few words?" Mr. Sanchez aborts the plan to speak, overwhelmed by the crowd of 40 present.

Fried chicken and cake are served, and the teachers are under strict orders to be served last because of a legitimate concern over short supplies. The two graduates with relatives attending each take a table for a family meal. Mr. Sanchez joins one of the families, but the teachers seclude themselves afraid to intermingle.

That night, as I recall the details to Annie, she brings up a valid question I hadn't previously thought about, being so enmeshed in the action. "Why do they have a valedictorian in prison?"

Day 123

Yesterday's demonstration of the proposed point card was quietly received during afternoon roll call. I boiled down the instructions to six necessary PowerPoint slides on the front side of a handout and used the back to write out examples on a sample point card. My strategy was to have the material quickly understood and easily accessible. In total, my talking time didn't exceed ten minutes, and no questions were asked.

Bringing cookies again to make my message easier to swallow, I'm surprised by the liveliness of today's bunch. Several guards who weren't present yesterday are bold enough to refuse my one-page handout, and one makes it into a paper airplane, sending it flying through the room before the meeting is called to order. I'm thankful for the Juvenile Supervisor who calls the meeting to order. He delivers a few short notes before introducing me. My audience is held captive by the presence of their supervisor. By the looks of it, the JS is not my biggest fan but will not use this time to object.

Despite the blustery entrance, security falls in line with their leader, asking no questions and making no objections. I think all involved have sized me up and have concluded complaints are a waste because I have no power either way. Those with conviction will run it up the pole.

Day 126

Exhausted, I'm ecstatic for the weekend. To put a bow on training, I started the last two days two hours early and returned for the overnight shift last night. After spending roughly $70 on treats for the week, Annie helps me justify the expense and effort by highlighting the impact the experience will have on my portfolio and future employment. For now, I've made a dramatic improvement to the and helped the youth in our facility. Who knows; this may even be adopted by other juvenile facilities.

Counting down the seconds to 3:30, I look forward to the half-hour of compensatory time though, it doesn't come close to covering my extra clocked hours. As I relaxedly reflect while returning from the lunchroom, I notice the airy blustering of fluffy flakes out our solitary, second-story hallway window. Aside from the two opaque, ovular marks made from scraping off etched graffiti, it is a wistful, picturesque scene. Several sprawling hills with wild grasses and trails ebb over the barbed wire. At times, deer can be seen prancing in the freedom of untouched landscape. Today, the view is straight out of a snow globe. The downy mist weightlessly floats in every direction, up, down, horizontal, fading, growing, and swirling before touching down and disappearing.

Wanting to share the serenity, I poke my head in the tutoring door. "Ms. Arnold, there is quite a winter wonderland out our bay windows." Ms. Arnold is the new volunteer coordinator. She is taller and full-figured but carries it well with an athletic strength. She has a kind face and eyes that listen. She is reserved in her new post (smart choice) and asks me questions in such a way as to not reveal her biases. Even as I expound in response, I cannot get a read on what she believes. She has an enigmatic, poker face. These types of people (the unreadables) cause me to proceed cautiously, so I extend a pine branch.

"Breathtaking," Ms. Arnold comments non-committally.

We stand captivatedly quiet, enjoying a rare moment of separation from the melancholy through a childlike wonderment. We each take a side next to the broad, fogged eggs that are centered in the windows.

I wait.

"It is truly wonderful, this view. I try to catch the deer grazing on the hill. I know they are there," she shares.

We wait.

Breaking the silence, "the view is almost perfect, save that debacle," I point to a large section of tilled grass.

"What do you suppose that is for?" Ms. Arnold wonders.

"That," I dramatically reveal, "is the farm! We are starting an agriculture program, and produce will TEEM from that section of overturned sod."

She perceives the cynicism. "You don't sound enthused?"

"Don't get me wrong. This facility has a rich history of being self-reliant." I put on my professor cap. "Pre-1970's we had large sections of farmland maintained by the boys: cows to milk, chickens for eggs, and a slaughterhouse. The only thing the facility imported was propane."

"So, why can't we get back to that?" She's still idyllically hopeful of the impact her department can have on lost youth. "I think a little hard work could be good for the boys."

"A little manual labor would work miracles," I agree. "Idle hands are what got them into this mess. Wear 'em out. Teach them real work and build a skill. But, we're doing it in all the wrong ways."

"How so?" I've captured her interest. Every fresh face to this institute, including myself, is caught off guard by the dysfunction surrounding, but not necessarily caused by, these young men.

"Well," pulling back the incompetent curtain, "they tilled an area of about 50 feet by the size of a football field. That is . . ."

"Oh, I'm not good at math," Arnold interjects perturbed.

". . . 15,000 square feet of farmland. We don't even have a teacher."

"I have a girlfriend who just retired from teaching incarcerated youth a horticulture program in a greenhouse," Ms. Arnold connects. "She said it made all the difference."

"I wholeheartedly agree. Planting, nurturing, harvesting; heck, we can even have the same kids cook their produce as part of the meals for the facility. Have them scooping and serving and soaking in the accolades. We could put their names on a placard and have the Warden come down to shake their hands for a picture. But, that won't happen. Not this way." I pause to take a breath and make my point in the most composed fashion. As skeptical as I've become, I still hold out hope that the fates will tilt in our favor and turn this place around. "They should have started with a 15 by 20 foot plot. I would relish taking my second period class down. That way we could use the time connected to lunch dismissal. Five or so kids could create the product from start to finish. We could take the season to let the hype build, and the low supply will heighten more kids' desire to belong. The program could grow from there."

Ms. Arnold critiques my plan. "But, that garden wouldn't feed many people."

I attempt to explain the nuances of delicately modifying behavior to achieve the most prosperous results. "The first year culminating in one meal is all that would be needed to publicize the program. Anything more would outreach our grasp. Kids would have the winter cooped up to stew and yearn for the outdoors. The next year, we could have more plots and make a competition between the houses. Madison grows tomatoes, and Washington grows cucumbers. The competition creates pride, drive, and positive self-worth."

"Well, why can't we have that now?" Ms. Arnold's unwavering belief in Goodness has yet to be tarnished by this experience.

"It has been overdone upfront. The bar has been set inordinately high and, thus, is doomed to fail similarly to the computer classrooms." I try to reveal the inner workings of ineffectualness. "Opening one classroom with kids who wanted to be in it and could responsibly handle it would've let them experience success and spread the word. Lower the supply and increase the demand." I offer a simplified strategy. "Instead, we haphazardly shove 60 plus kids in with undertrained teachers, and the mess ensues. With this plot, we have a large piece of earth that needs to be turned and seeded in about six months and no teacher. I'm sure the job description will also include maintaining the five dilapidated greenhouses as well. In order to do this, we need at least 40 willing kids as a start-up, which we don't have. And even if there is a miraculously qualified person sent down from heaven to be at this facility, the tedium of the application process will surely weed them out."

"You don't sound like you're hopeful, upbeat self when it comes to this issue," Ms. Arnold seems more concerned than disappointed.

"I have faith for miles," I reassure, "but around here, you have to be realistic. Each of these kids needs 20-50 people to intervene in their lives to right the ship. It took at least that many to screw them up. I'm just one man willing to send them in the right direction, and I hope, hope, hope and pray that others will find these youth, and that the youth are willing to receive the help." I tear up with the revelation of my mission. "The outlook is bleak."

"Sounds like you've given up before this has a chance to happen." Now, I've let her down. "That's not very positive."

"Positive and realistic don't have to be polar opposites. Is it possible? Yes. Is it likely? It is more likely that someone will be struck by lightning while holding a winning lottery ticket." I chuckle but return to serious to impart the moral of this lesson. "I impact what I have the ability to impact. The rest I have to leave to the brokenness. For my health and effectiveness, I control my own universe, and that's all. When I see the chance to make a difference, I take a stab. If everyone else did the same, things might be different."

A long silence calms the building tensions. We tranquilly take in our last look at the pure brushstrokes.

"Well, we will see. We will see," Ms. Arnold ends our discussion in a vague, sing-songy way. The painting continues as we drift back to our posts.

Day 127

The day is finally HERE!!! I excitedly dread the implementation of my creation. I saw something through from start to the finish, and it is currently being piloted throughout the institution as I walk through the gate.

Cautiously observing as security escorts youth through the halls of the school, I aim to evaluate the atmosphere. The guards give nothing up, and as class starts, I come to realize it's just another day. All the corporate meetings and trainings were just public forums to air grievances. Not a soul has the gumption or fortitude to impede the transition.

Casually monitoring the student's progress through Virtual Education, my attention is intermittently drawn to my email. I figure if I can put out the sparks before they blaze, this point card will become the new normal.

When my focus returns to the youth, Charles Wilson is detailing his entrepreneurial spirit. "We got nickel and dime bags. Hell, I'm the only guy in my hood who sells dubs. Me and my boys pullin down two gees a week. Two grand each."

Wilson is partially attending to his workstation, so I attempt a soft redirect to keep the group on-task. "Mr. Wilson, I appreciate that you are working while you talk. Can we please keep the conversations appropriate?"

Wilson looks hurt. "Man, stop buggin us."

Reconsidering the original interruption, I try to smooth things over. "Like I said, the class is working hard, which I appreciate. Please refrain from talking about drugs."

"Why?" He is genuinely confused.

If the entire culture and lifestyle of the neighborhood where this young man grew up has normalized the trafficking of drugs, I'm unsure how to refute a message so deeply engrained. "Because, that's probably what got you here."

"See, now you making shit up," Wilson exclaims. "I'm here on gun charges."

I'm in deep. This discussion has drawn the class' attention. I pull a thread to see if I can make a connection for the boys. "So, why did you feel you needed to carry a gun?"

"Man," wiping my question away with his hand, "we rollin deep as fuck! That's why." He volleys back to me.

"I'm assuming that means you have a lot of money or expensive merchandise on you, and you feel there is a need to protect it. When you get involved with illegal activities, you get pulled deeper and deeper." I try to turn the tables, "How old is the oldest drug dealer you know?"

He cautiously answers, "In their twenties," suspicious of a trap.

Sincerely, I inquire, "What happens to most of them?"

"They end up in jail or shot." The lightbulb has gone off for Wilson. "Oh, oh, I got you, Masters."

Bringing it home, "I'm not trying to rag on you guys. You're all doing great work today. But, if I care about you, I can't let you keep talking about things that will end poorly." I've captured their attention; the remolding can begin. "We have some holidays coming up. What's your fondest family gathering memory?"

Wilson appreciates the investment I've made in him and will humor me. "My family does reunions at the local hall every summer. We barbeque, get drunk, dance, smoke up. Last year, some opps threw a brick through the window. Me and my boys tracked them down and beat their ass." He gets an affirming handclasp from his neighbor."

The conversation had a promising start, but the baseline life of these kids is tragic. I don't want to discourage them, so I try to find the silver lining. "Who cooks when your family gets together?"

"My grandma and my O G."

"What is an 'O G'?" I need a street dictionary.

"Original gangster. My mom," he explains.

"Next time," I suggest, "sit between your mom and grandma, and when they're finished eating, offer to take their plates, so they can sit and enjoy."

Revelation fills Wilson's face. The class remains silent for several minutes as they picture how much joy and pride this simple act of service would bring to the women they love.

The day passes without a wisp of protestation. Though I know the battle has just begun, I take solace in my quiet victory today, knowing the hard work is behind me. My baby is being carried throughout Boys Home. The road ahead is winding and bumpy with tweaks and modifiers, but I'm doubtful that my work will get repealed. I take a cleansing breathe and feel confident I will be equipped for each battle as they come.

"Bitch, I'm off probation! Ba Ba Bitch, I'm off probation!" Mrs. Peters joins me in a two-step shuffle as we rap the way to our cars. At the start of shift tomorrow, I'll be a fully tenured, vested employee of the state.

In the public school system, it can take two to four years to earn the protection tenure provides. Days are admittedly tougher behind bars, and as a perk for not running off the job, pulling my hair, and screaming, my position is now relatively secure. Based on the stories and rumors, I'd have to no-call, no-show for several days in a row or be caught with my pants down on the job to be fired. It may not be the easiest or best job, but I feel secure. With an addition to my family rapidly approaching, that is all I can hope for now.

Epilogue

If the reader has an unsatisfied feeling, that's to be expected. I wrote this book to illustrate a condition of the American Dream that hasn't been worked through. We sugar coat, sweet talk, and throw "positive" programming at delinquent children while setting them up to fail worse than they already have in the past. Our system makes the involved youth feel warm during their stay, but like most treats, leaves them with a bad aftertaste because the euphoria is unsustainable. The solution is to take a fresh look with a new set of eyes. We need leaders who understand the systemic issues that cause mass incarceration (broken homes, generational poverty, and a lack of rights and opportunities) and address them at the root. Once the problem is defined, we need to collaboratively develop a plan with foresight of any implications for future generations.

The rub is the never-ending, instantaneous stimulus of the internet age has engrained us to do what feels good in the moment and tackle any consequences long after the point of no return. If you are passionate, engage people in tough discussions. Don't blather on about what you think in-person or online. Continually have uncomfortable back-and-forth dialogues that may end in disagreement but also mutual edification. Only when the taboo is carefully removed can truth start to emerge.

Thank you for reading my story. It is truly a humble honor to have your patronage.

Acknowledgements

First and foremost, I want to thank each and every person who took the time to read my drafts. Your encouragement and advice was invaluable during the writing process.

I want to thank my family. You built and nurtured the foundational drive I have to continually better myself and the world around me.

I want to thank my in-laws. Your light-hearted, care-free gatherings have been the respite that empowered me to keep going.

I want to thank my roommate. Your creative vision gives this book opening allure.

I want to thank my children. You will never fathom how much love and joy you've brought your mother and me.

I can't thank my wife enough. Your patiently crafted corrections and musings made this book complete.

All praise and honor be to the transcendent God of all created things. Despite my failings, You sacrificed to be in communion with me.

Copies of this story and the E-reader version can be found on amazon.com.

Contact the author: jon.k.masters@gmail.com